New Understandings of Administration

HARLEIGH B. TRECKER

NEW UNDERSTANDINGS
OF ADMINISTRATION

ASSOCIATION PRESS • NEW YORK

Table of Contents

v

Introduction

A NEW BOOK on administration should offer to its readers guidance, stimulation, new insights, and challenge. It should suggest better ways of getting work done with and through people. Such is the intention and purpose of this book.

Administration of the community services is a major concern of many agencies today. Administrators are asking such questions as: How can we develop a more efficient organization where communication will be clear, rapid, and effective? How can we speed up the decision-making processes within the framework of our democratic philosophy? How can we clarify the roles and responsibilities of professional workers and administrative volunteers? How can we work out the proper allocation of responsibility between the central office and the various branches or divisions of our program? Can we do a better job of delegating responsibilities and make certain that persons who have accepted these responsibilities are held accountable?

In this book a look is taken at some of these questions and at a number of others. The book has as one of its goals the relating of some important selected findings from current study and research to the practice of administration. An effort is made to summarize new knowledge of individual and group behavior, organization theory, motivation and leadership. Theory formulations from business administration, public administration, and educational administration are examined. Throughout the book new learnings from the past decade are evaluated and efforts are made to apply these learnings to the day-to-day tasks of administration.

The focus of the book is the administrator, that is, the executive and other persons who have primary responsibility for giving leadership to the operation of the community service agency or to a part of it. In addition, it is believed that administrative volunteers such as agency presidents and key officers and committee chairmen who share responsibility with professional workers in many agencies will find helpful material which will enable them to perform their duties more competently. It is hoped, also, that the book will encourage these administrative leaders to do further study and to make use of additional material.

The book concentrates upon community service agencies that are generally identified with the broad field of social welfare. Special emphasis is placed on those agencies that are led and administered by both professional workers and volunteer workers who work together as leadership teams. Furthermore, they have a structure and organization which is deliberately designed to provide for a maximum amount of participation by appropriate people in the affairs of the agency. Also, many of the agencies have both central and branch operations. It is to be hoped, also, that this book will be valuable to many others in the field of community service even though their agencies may be organized somewhat differently.

Part One, New Understandings of Administration, has four chapters, the first of which points up some of the challenges faced by administrators today. Chapter 2 offers an overview of administration as a total process. Chapters 3 and 4 focus upon what must be understood about the agency and the community. Part Two, Skill in Administration, has eight chapters. This material is operational or job focused. Chapter 5 deals with the function and role of administrators. Chapter 6 covers what is involved in establishing and improving communication. Chapter 7 is devoted to the processes of planning and co-ordination. Boards, committees, and agency members are discussed in Chapter 8. Work with the staff is reviewed in Chapter 9. Chapter 10 is concerned with evaluating the effectiveness of administration, and Chapter 11 is given over to executive development programs. The final chapter sketches patterns for progress on the new frontiers of administration.

Throughout the volume brief illustrations are offered from time to time. These have been drawn from actual records kept by administrative leaders and from notes of conferences, institutes, etc. Every effort has been made to disguise these examples so that they will not be personally revealing. To this end, editorial changes have been made and certain pieces of material have been combined with other pieces of material.

At the conclusion of the book a selected bibliography of reading references is offered for those who wish to do further study.

A great many people have been involved in this book. The writer has had many years of teaching in the field of social administration plus many years of administrative experience. He has been helped by countless students who have participated with him in various projects. He has had the pleasure of working with many executives from local, state, and national agencies as a consultant, institute leader, conference chairman, or study director. Special appreciation must be given to the Community Division of the National Board of the YWCA because this division provided a considerable amount of material for the book. The writer served with the Division as consultant for a two-year study project on administration. This provided him with an excellent opportunity to test out some of his theoretical formulations and it gave him the stimulation of working with many splendid administrators who provided much illustrative material from their carefully kept case records. Thus, many people have had a part in this work. However, the author is, of course, solely responsible for the material selected and presented. It is to be hoped that these words will be helpful to many administrators who are striving for new insights and new understandings of their task.

Harleigh B. Trecker

West Hartford, Connecticut

PART ONE

ADMINISTRATION: PURPOSE AND PROCESS

CHAPTER 1

New Challenges to Administration

ADMINISTRATORS EVERYWHERE are facing sharp new challenges today. In the community service or social welfare field these challenges are especially pointed. Executives, department heads, division directors, and their related board and committee leaders are assessing the impact of changing times on the administrative process. Earnest questioning is being directed toward prevailing practices. Thoughtful analyses of critical problems are being made. Administrators are reviewing their jobs in an effort to deepen understandings and to formulate new and better ways of work. There seems to be a growing conviction that improvement can be made and that new insights regarding administrative skill and competence can be realized. Thus the challenges are being met with vigor, courage, and energy.

15

Great Community Changes

Great community changes have had their impact on the human service agencies and the ways they are administered. Well known is the tremendous growth of population and the especially large numbers of children and youth and older persons who require specialized community services. In addition, there has been a striking movement of population from rural to urban areas. There has been an increase in the number of large metropolitan areas and a substantial shift of population from the central cities out to suburban communities. Along with this has been the surge toward urban renewal and redevelopment, which has changed the nature of vast sections of the central city. Networks of new highways have changed the map in many places and distances have shrunk remarkably.

When one examines the pattern of work or employment, it is clear that more women are at work today and that many young people are having a difficult time finding their place in the work of society. There are apparently fewer employment opportunities for unskilled workers and increasing need for the highly skilled. Despite the shorter working week there is an increased productivity and a general rise in the standard of living. This rise, however, is uneven and a considerable number of families still find themselves in sharply restricted circumstances.

Many new needs and problems have arisen and for the most part the problems of today are complex ones and are interrelated. More organizations, agencies, and services have been established to deal with these problems. Governmental agencies and voluntary agencies have increased, and in the governmental field the various levels of government are frequently involved in financing and in rendering service. One of the major debates today centers around ways of meeting human needs and providing human services. A central question seems to be what is the responsibility of the public sector of the economy and what is the responsibility of the private sector?

Changes in the Agency

During the past several decades some community agencies have grown very large. They have great capital investments and large operating budgets. They must employ large staffs to carry on their operations and, in addition, they need an increasing number of volunteer workers. These large agencies with substantial capital holdings, large staffs, and large operating budgets have a considerable number of management problems as they strive to use their resources efficiently.

In the large cities and in the metropolitan areas, many agencies have established branches or units of their program out in the newer communities in an effort to provide service to new populations. The so-called decentralized programs removed from the center of the agency have created problems of authority and delegation of responsibility. In addition, it should be pointed out that some agencies are operating with old—even worn out—facilities which are poorly located in relation to population. Some of these agencies are seeking to discover where they should locate their work and what kind of new facilities they should have. As one compares the community today with that of fifty years ago, it is obvious that there are many more agencies and many more services. Many of the services are specialized or partial in scope and this growth of such services has brought with it the need for co-ordination and joint planning.

There has been a substantial growth in professionalization, but at the same time there has been a mounting shortage of professionally trained personnel. Standards of service and good practice have been formulated and recognized, but because of the personnel shortage it has been difficult always to achieve these standards.

Challenges to Administration

Many administrators in recent years have felt a sense of urgency and pressure as they endeavor to give leadership to the work of their agencies. They are finding that they must achieve greater clarity as to their purposes and must use their sense of purpose more explicitly in program and service choices. Along with this, they must become more selective as to the clientele they will endeavor to serve, and this is especially important in the voluntary agency realm as they strive to secure the necessary support and resources. Administrators are conscious of their responsibility to do a better job of interpretation and public relations so that the community will understand the contribution they are trying to make. This community understanding, however, must be achieved in relation to a total community planning approach. Administrators are doing more work with other agencies both from the standpoint of planning and operation. They find that they must be concerned about broad public programs and must be more active in the realm of social legislation.

Many administrators are giving serious thought to questions of structure and organization so that they may have more efficient and more rapid communication. They are looking at their ways of work and are reviewing the decision-making process with sharper questioning as to who must be involved in the making of decisions. Decentralization of service has brought with it the need to understand the processes of delegation and the processes of assigning responsibility with accountability.

In an era of personnel shortage, both professional and volunteer, it is clear that much thought is given to the better organization, utilization and direction of manpower efforts. The roles and responsibilities of volunteers and professionals are being reviewed, with considerable attention being given to the process of policy formulation as contrasted with the process of policy implementation. Many agencies are giving thought to the evaluation of their program and services and one finds a large number of agency and community studies under way.

Administrators are recognizing the fact that they are being called upon to fulfill a larger leadership role. At the same time, they are conscious of the need to define more specifically the essential skills and competencies needed in administration today. Although they are pressed and loads are frequently burdensome, they are thinking about the need for executive development programs not only to improve their own on-the-job skills but somehow to locate the potential administrators for the future.

Thus, as the tempo of life quickens, as the need for and tasks of administration grow greater and greater, and as management problems mount in all community agencies, it has become essential that critical analyses be made of the administrative process. The National Board of the YWCA through its Community Division carried on a two-year study project in the area of administration. The project involved nineteen YWCAs located in various cities. It was set up to provide an organized and orderly approach or method for professional and volunteer workers to use in studying their own practices. It was designed to help persons to locate and understand the problems encountered in administering a YWCA. It was believed that through self-study it would be possible to determine more precisely the administrative skills required by persons who occupied leadership positions. Another goal was to determine some of the principles of administration that seemed particularly pertinent to the YWCA.

In studying their work professional and volunteer workers co-operated as leadership teams and kept records on selected units of work for periods of three to six months. Periodic workshops of the participants brought them together for face-to-face discussions, during which problems were formulated and recorded material analyzed. While it grew out of the setting of the YWCA, it should be of value to all administrators who work in the human service field. In the chapter which follows, the nature and purpose of administration will be discussed in a kind of frame of reference or overview.

CHAPTER **2**

Administration—An Overview

Administration is a process of working with people in ways that release and relate their energies so that they use all available resources to accomplish a purpose, such as that of providing needed community services and programs. People, resources, and purposes are thus brought together by administration in a continuous, dynamic process.

A clear understanding of the nature and purpose of administration is of great importance. Recent descriptive definitions are helpful and valuable as one endeavors to get an overview. Some of the current definitions which seem particularly pertinent are presented below.

Spencer observes that administration "is the conscious direction of the internal relationships and activities of the enterprise toward the achievement of goals. . . . Administration is also seen as the conscious intervention in the interacting forces operating between the agency and the larger community of which it is a part. . . . The administrative process is essentially the same in all human enterprises, it includes determination of goals, securing the resources, determination of policies and standards of service, allocation of resources in accordance with a work plan, maintenance of operation so as to produce the desired kind and amount of service, evaluation, and accounting for the use of resources."[1]

Tead sees administration as, "the direction of people in association to achieve some goal temporarily shared. It is the inclusive process of integrating human effort so that a desired result is obtained."[2]

In another discussion Tead says, "Administration is the comprehensive effort to direct, guide and integrate associated human strivings which are focused toward some specific ends or aims. . . . Administration is conceived of as the necessary activities of those individuals (executives) in an organization who are charged with the ordering, forwarding and facilitating the associated efforts of a group of individuals brought together to realize certain defined purposes."[3]

Public assistance administration is reported to consist of a number of processes. Wilkins says, "The administrative processes utilized to assure progressively improved public assistance services are program analysis and planning, policy formulation, procedural implementation, interpretation of program objectives and needs, supervision, consultation, staff development and management and fiscal controls. Dynamic administration also encompasses the

22

development of recommendations for legislative change based on a continuing evaluation of agency services."[4]

Tebow observes in addition that, "These processes are interrelated and simultaneously operated. The effectiveness of each is dependent on each of the others and on the co-ordination of the different processes into the whole process of administration."[5]

An educational association concludes that, "Administration, then, may be defined as the total of the processes through which appropriate human and material resources are made available and made effective for accomplishing the purposes of an enterprise. It functions through influencing the behavior of persons."[6]

In these and other definitions it is evident that administration is seen as a *process of working with people* to establish and maintain a system of co-operative effort so as to provide services. This way of looking at administration implies a wide distribution of responsibility throughout the whole agency. Thus, many people have administrative duties. Some people, namely, executives and certain others have primary responsibility for administrative leadership. They must understand that administration as a process has two important dimensions. *First,* there is the dimension of the task, the project, the assignment, or the problem upon which people are working. *Second,* there is the psycho-social dimension of feelings released by these people as they work on their tasks. It is the release of energy and feeling properly channeled and directed by administrative leaders which enables people to accomplish their tasks in relation to the goal of agency service. The idea of process carries with it the notion of movement. Movement means that people work on their assignments step by step and in a systematic, planned, orderly manner. In this view of administration it is assumed further that the steps of analyzing situations, of securing agreement among people, of making decisions in the midst of several alternatives, and of the carrying out of decisions are interwoven and interrelated.

Of great significance is the assumption that administration is primarily a matter of establishing effective working relationships with and between people. Getting work done to accomplish agency purposes is basically a matter of motivating people to their finest and highest levels of achievement. The effectiveness of administration must be judged by the simultaneous consideration of two major criteria. *First,* how well the purposes of the agency are being achieved; and *second,* the extent to which the people who are engaged in carrying forward the work of the agency grow in skill and competence. Thus, in good administration ends and means are inseparable.

As we examine this approach to administration in detail it is important that the frame of reference behind it and the central ideas which underlie it be presented.

Some Central Ideas about Administration

First, the work of agencies is carried on by *task groups of people* working together to fulfill assignments, solve problems, make decisions, recommend and act on legislation, create policy, determine procedures, develop programs, and provide services. Some of these task groups are or may be the agency members, the board, the committee of management, various other committees, the staff, and special groups. Some of these groups are regularly established by virtue of the agency constitution. Some groups are special groups that have been set up to deal with special assignments. Each task group, whether it is regular or special has authority, responsibility, and limits as granted to it by the agency constitution or by the creating authority. These administrative task groups must be understood in their similarities and in their differences.

Second, the groups mentioned above require *leadership* to get their work done. None of these groups is a leaderless group. All of them require the efforts of people particularly trained and particularly competent to enable them to fulfill their tasks. These administrative leaders may be professional workers or volunteer workers depending upon the agency. Ordinarily, the chief administrative leader is the agency executive on the professional side and the agency president or chairman on the lay side.

Third, administrative leadership to these task groups is given by *leadership teams.* The primary leadership team consists of the professional worker and the volunteer worker. Here for example, the executive director and the agency president team up to give leadership to a variety of task groups. Or, in another instance, an agency staff member and a committee chairman may work together as a team on a particular assignment. If the agency is metropolitan in scope and has a number of branches or district officers, the branch director and the branch chairman constitute one team. A number of other combinations can be visualized, and in certain instances several leadership teams of several groups may be working together. The way the leadership team functions is crucial to the success of the work of the agency.

The professional worker and the volunteer worker have different responsibilities and different roles to fulfill as they give administrative leadership. These roles and responsibilities must be defined and understood. Generally, the volunteer role is major in such areas as over-all policy making; staff role is major in staff supervision, program performance, and in direct services to individuals and groups. These roles are related to particular assignments in particular situations and as the work of the task group proceeds the role of the administrative leader shifts and changes. Some leadership teams, particularly the metropolitan agency executive director and the metropolitan board president, carry very broad responsibilities. A center director and chairman, who must necessarily be more focused upon the problems of their particular center rather than the city as a whole, have less responsibility.

In all cases, however, effective team work is based upon commonality of goal, understanding of the role and work of the other person, ability to communicate or share material, and mutual respect and regard for one another.

Fourth, in some agencies there are *many task groups and leadership teams at work* on assignments, problems, or jobs at the same time. Some of these tasks may include developing personnel policies and practices, preparing the budget, establishing a new service in a new community, creating a more effective membership organization, developing policies for special new programs and so forth. No matter what the task or assignment, in every case certain basic questions have to be raised:

1. What is the task? Is it a matter of policy making, procedure formulation, or program development? The nature of the task must be defined and understood.

2. Whose task is this? Where does it belong? The task must be assigned to the appropriate group or to an individual to carry it out.

3. When should this assignment be done and how must it be carried on in relation to other assignments in the agency? Thus, great attention must be given to timing.

4. What are the specific goals of this task assignment? What are the definitions of limits to the task? It is important that thought be given to the authority and responsibility which have been assigned to the work group.

5. What kinds of material will this task group have to have in order to make an intelligent decision?

In all of the questions listed above, administrative judgment is essential.

After answering these questions, administrative leadership teams must then work with task groups and their individual members in carrying through the task or in handling the assignment. This is essentially the over-all process of administrative leadership. Here it is important that the professional worker and the volunteer worker define their specific responsibilities and their specific roles. Working with the task group goes through a series of steps, and must be understood in relation to a time schedule. Each session of the task group produces more work assignments for individuals and groups. The next session of the task group grows out of the work that it has done to date. The role and responsibility of the leadership team must be redefined as new needs arise. Some tasks can be completed very quickly; others take much longer. Some tasks require much more help from the administrative leadership team than others.

Fifth, since there are many task groups at work simultaneously, it is necessary to arrange them into a formal *organization or structure* which will show them as being related to and in communication with each other. Continuous communication is essential if groups are to work together. Since these many groups who are at work on many tasks are likely to be at different stages in their work and since they are operating in different functional areas, their efforts must be *co-ordinated.* The task of providing leadership for the co-ordination and integration of activity is a primary one in the portfolio of the executive director and the agency president. In addition, all of related leadership teams must seek to co-ordinate their work with the other ongoing groups.

Sixth, as the many task groups carry forward their work it is necessary for them to make *decisions* and prepare reports. After this, action must be taken and then implementation of decisions is required. Under these conditions the question of when to report, to whom to report, and to whom to assign the follow-up of the decision looms large. Here again the chief executive carries a major responsibility.

Major Understandings Needed by Administrators

What do administrators need to know and understand as they assume and carry forward their important administrative leadership duties? Clearly, many things could be listed in answer to this question. The following key areas of understanding have been selected because they represent major items which are of great importance.

First, administrators must understand *the agency itself.* Those who would give leadership to its work must have a deep and growing understanding of its purposes, its goals, and its service area. They must be familiar with the clientele that the agency serves and must be conscious of the specific needs of this clientele. They should have knowledge of the agency's history because the present is always related to the past and the future likewise grows out of both the present and the past. Administrators need to be clear about the agency philosophy, values, and beliefs. They must know and understand the ways of work of the agency. They must know what resources are available for utilization and what additional resources are needed. They must be clear on agency policies, procedures, and program. They must have an awareness of the agency's lacks and shortcomings and must be conscious of the points where improvement is needed. Most important, they must have a sense of agency wholeness and totality inasmuch as their primary responsibility is directly concerned with this over-all operation.

Administrative leaders must have a deep understanding of *agency purposes and goals.* Furthermore, they must make wise and continuous use of their understanding of purpose. Purpose is their primary point of reference. It influences and guides every move that the administrator makes. The administrator must give creative focus to this purpose because purpose is the motivating force of all human effort. Unfortunately, in the past some administrators have failed to give enough time to this matter of goal determination. As Selznick has put it, "Once an organization becomes a 'going concern,' with many forces keeping it alive, the people who run it can readily escape the task of defining its purposes. This evasion stems partly from the hard intellectual labor involved, a labor that often seems but to increase the burden of already onerous daily operation."[7] Thus, if it is not to default in a major way, administrative leaders must be concerned with goal determination and purpose clarification. It is difficult to concentrate on purpose, but it is essential.

Second, since every agency is always a part of a *community,* administrators must have a substantial amount of understanding of the forces which are operating in the community where the agency exists. They must know and understand a great deal about the history of their community and the forces at work on the contemporary scene. They should know about the population make-up and the economic developments. They should be concerned about cultural, ethnic, and other special population characteristics. They should understand the basic structure of the community and should understand the processes through which the community goes as it makes its decisions. They should be alert to new needs that are arising in the changing community and they should endeavor to make planful use of community data of a sociological kind. They should, of course, be familiar with the other agencies in their service realm and they should understand the basic community planning processes that are at work.

Third, administrative leaders must understand how to help to provide an *organized work environment.* As noted earlier, the agency is made up of many groups of people. These groups are dynamic, evolving, and changing. The members of these groups bring into their work situation their deep needs for status, recognition, and growth. It is necessary to organize these various groups into a system of co-operative effort so that they will be seen and felt as working together. Organization is a process of so relating people to each other that they function at their maximum capacity. Organization charts are merely visual aids. Organization charts do not develop an organized work environment. Only when people feel that their needs and goals are being met can we have an effective human organization. Furthermore, people must feel that their efforts and their contributions help the agency to arrive at these goals. What makes an organized work environment? What kind of a work atmosphere will contribute to productivity and satisfaction? One thing that is very certain is that the way administrative leaders themselves work is a very important part of work environment or atmosphere. When administrators are well organized in their work this seems to carry over to the work groups. When the administrator pays attention to the creation of a climate or atmosphere which is essentially free, and at the same time challenging and vigorously directed, people then have a better chance to participate, to respond, and to produce.

Fourth, administrative leaders must understand how to facilitate *communication* within the organization. Ronken and Lawrence indicate that this is a major part of the job of the administrator when they say, "The administrator needs primarily to be concerned with the facilitating of relationships and communication in his organization. This is a different way of thinking about the job of administration from one that is commonly encountered. Administrators frequently think of their jobs as being one of solving problems, formulating policy, making decisions, delegating authority and checking up to make sure that their subordinates are living up to their delegated responsibility. It follows, from this concept of the job, that they spend considerable time in making value judgments about their subordinates and trying to find the individual who was to blame for something that went wrong, in giving orders to subordinates and in trying to please their superiors so that they will make favorable judgments. On the other hand, could not the administrator more usefully hold the following assumptions about his job: I am best performing my job when I am maintaining the conditions for clear and candid communications and working relationships with my assistants. If I am doing my job well, it will follow that my associates and I, in fact, will be spending our time defining, clarifying and solving our mutual problems. Instead of thinking it was up to him, the administrator, to supply the answers, the administrator would then be searching with others for answers in the situation itself."[8]

Fifth, administrative leaders must be concerned in a major way with establishing *effective working relation-*

ships with and between the many people who carry forward the tasks of the agency. As Glover and Hower state the case, "We conceive of the administrator as being confronted with and as being a part of constantly changing situations which are always unique, always related to the past and to the future. What the administrator may usefully do about one situation today is unlikely to be appropriate in the situation as it will have evolved tomorrow or in another situation also unique which has a different past and a still different future. The administrator may start as planned but what follows thereafter depends upon the successive reactions that the administrator encounters and what the administrator himself does in response to these reactions."[9] How the administrator behaves, works with and relates to people, clearly affects the kinds of behavior responses he gets back from people. The way the administrator behaves and his perception, understanding, and sensitivity toward the behavior of the people in the situation are interrelated. What the administrator sees in the situation, his judgment, and his inferences about it tend to influence his behavior. Inasmuch as individuals and groups change, the administrator must redefine his role as changes occur. His primary moves and subsequent directions are determined not in prearranged sequence but in terms of where the people are and what they need from him and how well he is related to them. Effective administrators are persons who release the energy of people and help these people put their separate energies together so that they may be thought of as a united force.

Sixth, administrative leaders must understand the processes of *planning and co-ordinating.* Effective work with

staff and volunteers is always based upon a carefully conceived plan or design which has been quite thoughtfully
worked out. Planning is a matter of using considered and
thoughtful judgment in the place of haphazard and clut-
tered thinking or careless judgment. Effective planning
carries with it the notion that administrators are clear on
what their goals are and clear about the methods they will
follow in pursuit of those goals. The larger the organization, the more important is planning. Everyone who works
in large organizations labors under the disadvantage of
dealing with subjects or with areas that affect the whole
organization, yet being able to see only a part of it at any
one time. Therefore, administrative leadership teams must
take responsibility for bringing a sense of wholeness, integration, and totality to the enterprise. Since a considerable
variety of task groups must necessarily become engaged
in the solution of almost every administrative assignment
their acts cannot be isolated but must be taken in harmony
with the rest of the organization. When people become
engaged in planning together and in co-ordinating their
efforts under the leadership of administration there is
reason to believe that the individuals involved will often
experience a sharp sense of discovery and a new awareness
of the many dimensions and outreaches of the agency.

Seventh, administrative leaders must understand how to
facilitate change within their agency. As Sorenson and
Dimock have said, "Determined and persistent administrative leadership is required for planned institutional
change."[10] A number of studies have revealed the important role that administrative leaders must play if they
are to bring about positive and fundamental change in

their organizations. It has been pointed out that when there is deep conviction on the part of administrative leaders that this will help to bring about change throughout the whole agency. It has been observed that it is impossible to change just a piece of the agency without that change having an impact on the whole. There is evidence, too, that change in behavior can come only when people are involved, when they voluntarily see and understand the reasons for the change and then are encouraged to participate in making the decisions to change. As Ginsberg and Reilly have put it in their exploration of the principles and processes of change in large organizations, "Effective change is primarily a question of alteration in the behavior of various groups who carry major responsibility. Top management must recognize, therefore, that its success in carrying out major changes will largely depend on how well it mobilizes the psychological forces that can facilitate acceptance of the new and how well it diminishes those forces which reinforce people's adherence to the existing pattern. The major approaches available to management are effective communication, the control of anxiety, and the learning of new skills."[11]

Eighth, administrative leaders must understand the importance of their own *dynamic leadership role.* In addition to being enablers, they must exercise leadership. The modern administrator is more than a listener, more than an implementer, more than a policy server. He cannot always take a neutral position; he must give leadership to the other people who make up the agency. Selznick says, "It is the function of the leader statesman to define the ends of group existence, to design an enterprise distinctly adapted to these ends and to see to it that the design becomes a living reality."[12]

With vigor and directness Dimock states the case as follows: "Leadership requires a sense of accompanying responsibility; part of one's oath of trusteeship in institutional management is to lead, not merely to conform to the group average if such capitulation threatens institutional survival and the values one deeply believes in. . . . I am simply saying that leadership requires a higher sense of values, of intelligence, and of dedication than is expected of most people, simply because our institutions will retrogress if we are not able to command such people. . . . The leader has the obligation to discover better ways of building mouse traps, better ways of organizing and motivating, better ways of securing democratic leadership and of raising the level of performance and appreciation on the part of those in the organization which he happens to head. . . . One of the secrets of growth is an adequate challenge, a challenge that is both internal and external, self-imposed and outwardly imposed, higher administrators have a special responsibility for providing such challenges to those who are junior to them. . . . The greatest source of true efficiency both in the individual and in social institutions is derived from internal challenge and response."[13]

Therefore, administrative leaders must understand that it is their job to speak out when the facts reveal and substantiate serious unmet needs and service requirements. They must convey and express and utilize their knowledge as to standards of good practice. They must take a position regarding serious community issues. They must insist on having trained staff and adequate salaries for them. Administrative leaders must be critical, dissatisfied, and always searching for better ways of serving people. They must do more structuring and more planning and must take more initiative for carrying forward the major plans of the agency. Of tremendous importance is the fact that administrative leaders study their own work and evaluate their own methods. These evaluative acts on their part can set the tone for continuous agency appraisal.

Ninth, administrative leaders must understand that it is their responsibility to foster the *creative growth of persons.* What happens to people is of central importance. The behavior of administrators must be judged in terms of this ethical ideal. To what extent and to what degree does the practice of administration express recognition of the importance of people? To what extent and to what degree do we remember that we want to get the job done, but that another responsibility is that of helping the people who are doing the job develop their creative capacities? Administrative productivity is important, but of far greater importance is what happens to the individual in the process. As Hook has put it, the task of administration is "to make it possible for more and more people to become persons."[14] Clapp accents this thought when he says, "The highest service of administration is achieved in the realm of ideas, the products of the human mind. The will to think and think on purpose is the greatest asset a competent organization can possess. The creation of processes by which the will to think becomes the will to act with a sense of responsibility that attempts to assess the human consequences of its alternatives of decision is the object of the art and science of administration. The highest purpose of administration is to build processes which encourage and promote the growth of human talent, especially the talent to select progressively richer ends or goals and more effective means to achieve them."[15]

SUMMARY

To summarize the points made in this chapter—

1. Administration is work with people. It is a process based upon knowledge and understanding of human behavior, human relations, and human organization.

2. Administration is a process in which many persons share. Staff members, board members, agency members and clients, and the community must engage in or become involved in the over-all administrative process at points appropriate to their contribution and function.

3. The role of administrative personnel, no matter what job title they hold, is essentially that of enabling, helping, and leading so as to energize people toward the fulfilment of the objectives of the program.

4. The community service agency is the framework within which the administrative tasks are carried on. This agency framework inevitably conditions and controls the specifics of administrative process in a given situation.

5. In administration purposes, policies, and procedures are always related in a dynamic way and tend to become focused at the point of administrative action

and decision. Because agencies are whole and their parts interrelated, administration must be thought of as a whole process rather than as a series of segmented acts.

6. The quality of service rendered by the community service agency is definitely and explicitly affected by the kind of administration which the agency provides. Because of the inseparable nature of administration and service the quality of agency program is dependent in large measure upon the quality of agency administration.

7. The increasing magnitude of the service task places more and more emphasis upon the necessity of good administration. No matter how one views it, from the standpoint of cost or the standpoint of needs, community services are large and basic in society and must have competence in the administrative realm.

With the foregoing framework of ideas and understanding as a background it is now possible to take a more detailed look at the agency as a dynamic human organization. This material will follow in the next chapter.

NOTES

1. Sue Spencer, "The Nature of the Administrative Process in a Social Welfare Agency." Paper given at the Annual Forum, National Conference on Social Welfare, Atlantic City, N.J., June 6, 1960.

2. Ordway Tead, *Administration: Its Purpose and Performance* (New York: Harper, 1959), p. 2.

3. Ordway Tead, *The Art of Administration* (New York: McGraw-Hill, 1951), pp. 3–4.

4. Anne Wilkens, "Educational Needs of the Case Worker for Practice in the Field of Public Assistance: A Descriptive Statement of Professional Knowledge, Skills and Attitudes" (Washington, D.C.: U.S. Dept. of Health, Education, and Welfare, Social Security Administration, Bureau of Public Assistance and American Public Welfare Association, May 1958), p. 4.

5. Hilda P. Tebow, *Staff Development: An Integral Part of Administration* (Bureau of Public Assistance Report No. 35 [Washington, D.C.: U.S. Dept. of Health, Education, and Welfare, Social Security Administration, 1959]), pp. 1–2.

6. *Staff Relations in School Administration* (Washington, D.C.: American Association of School Administration, 1955), p. 17.

7. Philip Selznick, *Leadership in Administration* (Evanston, Ill.: Row, Peterson, 1957), p. 25.

8. Harriet O. Ronken and Paul R. Lawrence, *Administering Changes—A Case Study of Human Relations in a Factory* (Boston, Mass.: Harvard University, Division of Research, Graduate School of Business Administration, 1952), p. 315.

9. John B. Glover and Ralph M. Hower, *The Administrator* (Homewood, Ill.: R. D. Irwin, 1952), p. 4.

10. Roy Sorenson and Hedley S. Dimock, *Designing Education in Values* (New York, N.Y.: Association Press, 1955), p. 205.

11. Eli Ginsberg and Ewing W. Reilly, *Effecting Change in Large Organizations* (New York, N.Y.: Columbia University Press, 1957), p. 60.

12. Selznick, *Ibid.*, p. 37.

13. Marshall Dimock, *A Philosophy of Administration—Toward Creative Growth* (New York, N.Y.: Harper & Brothers, 1958), pp. 22–23.

14. Sidney Hook, "Bureaucrats Are Human," *The Saturday Review,* May 17, 1958, p. 41.

15. Gordon R. Clapp, "The Social Scientist and the Administrative Art," in Leonard D. White (ed.), *The State of the Social Sciences* (Chicago, Ill.: University of Chicago Press, 1956), p. 397.

CHAPTER **3**

Understanding the Agency

A̲DMINISTRATIVE LEADERS must have a deep and growing understanding of their agency as a human enterprise. In addition, they must help the people who work for or are served by it to understand it as a dynamic, changing entity with a history, purposes, and ways of getting work done. In this chapter an approach to understanding the agency will be presented. It is based on the premise that organizations are *people* and administration today must be people-centered.

As Greenwalt has said, "Organizations, corporate or otherwise, are not inanimate objects, composed of steel or brick or equipment, but living mechanisms made up of human beings. In whatever field an organization operates, it is nothing more than the total sum of the talents, the aspirations, and the characters of the human building blocks of which it is made, mellowed perhaps by the traditions and the collective experience left behind by other human beings who have gone before."[1] Along this same line Dubin says, "People give the dynamic quality to organizations. Organizations have buildings, capital equipment, inventories, and rules and regulations. But people make the organization go."[2] How these people are viewed and worked with is of major importance in creating an effective social agency. In most communities today there are many social agencies. In fact, there are many more agencies now than was true in an earlier period of history. Some of the agencies are financed and operated by government. Others are voluntary or private in organization and scope. Some provide a single highly specialized service and others are multiservice in that they do a variety of things and seek to meet a variety of needs.

It is interesting to contrast the stated purpose of a governmental welfare department with that of a private family service agency. The welfare department's purpose is: To administer the laws concerning assistance for the aged and the blind, aid to dependent children, and aid to the permanently and totally disabled, and laws concerning the welfare of children who require the care, protection, and discipline of the State; to collect for the support of persons in state institutions, to reimburse towns for a portion of their welfare expenditures, and to carry out other duties imposed by statute. The family service agency's purpose is: To help individuals achieve harmonious family interrelationships, gain self-understanding, attain healthy personalities and satisfactory social functioning through casework services. Differences in purpose such as noted above automatically suggest questions which must be answered by anyone who seeks to understand an agency.

1. What is the agency purpose and who decides what its purpose is?
2. Who does the agency serve and who decides this?
3. How is the agency financed?
4. How is the agency staffed?
5. How is the agency organized and how does it make decisions?
6. How is the agency administered and what are the roles and responsibility of its leaders?

One of the major differences among agencies is the way in which ultimate authority is determined. In the public field the elected representatives of the people have this authority entrusted to them for stated periods. Thus the Congress, the legislature, or the city council determines the broad goals of programs and provides the resources to implement them. Then the executive branch of the government carries out the program within the goals established. In the private field individual citizens who wish to sponsor and provide a particular service come together in association and with proper legal foundations. They set up a corporation, usually with a board of trustees or directors who make the major decisions as to policy and program. Then the board selects an executive to whom it delegates responsibility for operating the enterprise. The executive in turn is empowered to select staff necessary for the rendering of services.

In some voluntary agencies the *members* have the ultimate authority for the policy decisions. In the YWCA, for example, members are expected to share in and determine the major policies of the organization. These members are given the responsibility of electing the board of directors, to whom they may delegate the actual decision-making functions; however, the board is accountable to the members. In the membership agency, administration has a continuing charge to develop and create a strong, responsible, participating membership body. Members are considered to be the basic legislative arm of the agency, and the broader the base of participation the sounder is the legislative process. In a later chapter this way of work will be explored in greater detail.

The Agency—A Complex Social System

The modern social agency is a complex social system with many people involved in it. These include the board, administrative staff, other staff, volunteers, members, clients, or person served, and the supporting community. To bind all of these people together into a functioning whole is a major responsibility of administration.

As was stated in an earlier publication,[3] social agencies or social systems or multiple group organizations are sustained by the interaction of all who have a part in their creation and operation. Social agencies as social systems have certain characteristics which can be identified. They come into being and develop because certain common needs of people, personal and environmental, can best be met by organized community effort. Just as these agencies

44

are conceived by the community, they are continued and enabled to provide services because of the support the community gives to them.

These agencies have a variety of purposes expressed in social or human terms. To be of maximum value these purposes must be determined in relation to the other agencies and services available to people in meeting their needs. This implies the definite necessity for agencies to co-operate with others equally committed to similar goals.

These agencies render immediate service and meet contemporary needs, but they also have an inherent interest in shaping the future. The concern for the future, however, is concurrent with meeting the needs of the present. Directions for the future must emerge out of the critical evaluation of inadequacies in present services.

To understand the agency as a social system it must be seen as a whole because each part bears a relation to every other part and all are interdependent. The agency is a number of individuals organized into groups working together toward a common end. Each individual brings a different background and potential contribution. Each assumes a measure of responsibility for a part of the total agency job. Through the never ending process of personal communication and interaction between people, the agency actually comes into being. Though this can be expressed visually in organization charts showing relationships, the important outcome of the interaction of minds is the vitality of the sentiments, convictions, and influences developed among the participants as they render service.

Sayre supports this conception of the agency in his discussion of administration as a social process. He says that this view "centers its attention upon the organization as a social group, as a group of human beings each of whom brings to the organization his own unique set of values, attitudes, motives, personality structures—and it is the interaction of these individuals with each other which shapes the organization and determines its behavior far more than does the technology of the organization or its policies."[4]

In like terms Schoenfeld remarks that, "An agency is basically a complex web of human relationships. As a large-scale enterprise, it requires many persons to operate it skillfully. Such skill can be obtained and developed to its highest level only if there is early recognition on the part of all concerned that the co-ordination of each person's efforts is obtained only through the web of relationships created by the interdependence of all members of the organization."[5]

Caudill sees the hospital in similar terms when he says, "The hospital is a small society; the ongoing functioning of such a society affects the behavior of the people who make it up in many ways of which they are unaware. . . . Small society means a complex system of human interaction within which the performance of technical tasks takes place. . . . The behavior of people is in considerable part a function of the social setting within which they act."[6]

When the administrator sees the agency he administers as being (1) composed of individuals, who (2) work co-operatively in groups, (3) to achieve the shared purposes, of (4) providing services to meet human needs, he must try to understand *each* individual person in the agency setting.

The Individual in the Agency

Many people are required to operate the agency. Some are board members; others are on the professional staff. Still others volunteer their services in program leadership. Large agencies have hundreds of workers and even small agencies have all of the different types of personnel. As the administrator strives to understand the individuals who do the work of the agency he must ask: how do they understand the agency? what do they bring to it? how do they fit in? what is their commitment to the agency? what does the work mean to them and what is their motivation?

To create an effective staff or an effective board the administrator must develop good work groups and must understand how the individual fits into his work group. As Sayles says, "The individual's most immediate and meaningful experiences of work are obtained in the context of the work group. . . . Membership in the small group contributes directly to the shaping of attitudes and behavior toward the entire world of work."[7] Mayo supports this contention when he observes, "In industry and in other human situations the administrator is dealing with well-knit human groups and not with a horde of individuals. . . . Man's desire to be continuously associated in work with his fellows is a strong if not the strongest human characteristic. Any disregard of this by management or any ill-advised attempt to defeat this human impulse leads instantly to some sort of defeat for management itself."[8]

In addition it is important that the administrator understand that every individual has certain needs which he wants to meet in part through his work efforts. Argyris emphasizes this point. He says, "Healthy adults will tend to obtain optimum personality expression while at work if they are provided with jobs which permit them to be more active than passive, more independent than dependent, to have longer rather than shorter time perspectives, to occupy higher positions than their peers, to have control over their world, to express many of their deeper, more important abilities. These developmental trends may be considered as basic properties of the human personality. They are the givens that an administrator accepts the moment he decides to accept human beings as agents of the organization."[9]

In a recent discussion, Bennis likewise observes, "Individuals who come to work for an organization bring into the system some need which they desire to have satisfied on the job and certain expectations about the job they are to perform. On the other hand, the organization has certain needs to be fulfilled and a set of expectations to be fulfilled by the people who work for it. . . . The best leaders are those who capitalize on what other members of their organization can bring. It creates a more productive staff or group, inasmuch as this increased involvement creates higher motivation, usually leading to higher productivity. . . ."[10]

Clapp eloquently states the case for administrative leaders who both accept and understand individuals. He says, "Given two agencies with reasonable similarity in respect to the competence of its individual members, what makes one lethargic, pathetic, and erratic in its course and performance and the other purposive, energetic, and reasonably creative in its performance? I suspect that at the root of the causes may be found a fundamental difference in at least two respects—the presence or absence of a deep faith within the key administrators in the latent intellectual and emotional reasonableness of human beings and rejection or acceptance of the desire to reform people as contrasted with the willingness to let them reform themselves. I believe that one's beliefs and convictions about these two variables lie close to the heart of whatever may be the administrative art . . . A more limited and suggestive hypothesis might be something like this: The key to the performance of an organization is the positive willingness of individuals to spend and apply their energies, singly and in groups, to the tasks committed to their hands. How to elicit within and among the farthest reaches of an organization the positive self-induced desire, intent, and energy to decide to act is the central problem of administrative leadership."[11]

Skillful administrative leaders give individuals opportunities for creative growth in their jobs because they know individuals must grow if they are to become more productive in their work. In this illustration an executive shows interest in helping the volunteer chairman grow in comprehension of her job: "Since this was the first meeting of the group it was a feeling-out process—one of becoming acquainted and attempting to feel free to express themselves. There was some defensiveness on the part of some committee members. Even the staff present were not willing to admit openly their problems of work overload and so forth. The chairman did not fully understand the task at hand. Between now and the next meeting I hope to work with her and help her to get more comprehension of the job to be done."

An executive recognizes the growing ability of her team-mate: "It was agreed that my teammate would give the report to the board. She does this well and is growing constantly in her understanding of the total agency. I feel deeply that our progress in working together is dependent upon our sensitivity in providing easy, natural ways to know and appreciate each other as persons."

Formal and Informal Organization

The individual in the agency is always a part of two organizational systems, the formal and the informal. Administrators need to understand the characteristics of both types of organization as a further avenue for knowing the individuals and how they are fitting in and performing their tasks. Scholars of organization theory have in recent years spelled out the attributes of the formal and informal systems and have contrasted their impact on the persons involved.

As Redfield states, "A formal organization starts with a broad purpose or plan: this is subdivided into activities, and the activities are assigned to positions. Structural relationships are established between position A and position B, not between Mr. Smith and Miss Jones. . . . Every formal organization is built around a system of authority relationships, with each position superior or subordinate to other designated positions, as seen on an organization chart. Both parties to such a relationship acknowledge that the superior has power over the subordinate, even though the word 'boss' is never used. The relationship between a superior and a subordinate, and between a subordinate and a superior, is a central feature of formal organization structure. . . . When the initial organizational plan or purpose is subdivided, positions are grouped in various ways for the efficient accomplishment of subsidiary operations. This grouping of positions brings together not only positions but the people who man the positions."[12]

Argyris, in his discussion of formal organization, says, "The most basic property of formal organization is its logical foundation, essential rationality: man will behave rationally as the formal organization plan requires him to do."[13] In another place Argyris spells out some of the basic principles of formal organization as follows: *Task or work specialization*—organizational and administrative efficiency is increased by the specialization of tasks assigned to the participants of the organization. *Chain of command*—the principle of task specialization creates the plurality of parts, each performing a highly specialized task. However, a plurality of parts busily performing their particular objective does not form an organization. A pattern of parts must be formed so that the interrelationships among the parts creates the organization. Following the logic of specialization the planners create a new function, leadership, whose primary responsibility shall be the control, direction, and co-ordination of the interrelationships of the parts and to make certain that each part performs toward objectives adequately. Thus the assumption is made that administrative and organizational efficiency is increased by arranging the parts in a determinate hierarchy of authority where the part on top can direct and control the part on the bottom. *Unity of direction*—if the tasks of every person in a unit are specialized, the objective or purpose of the unit must be specialized. The principle of unity of direction states that administrative and organizational efficiency increases if each unit has a single activity (or homogeneous set of activities) that is planned and directed by the leader. *Span of control*—the principle of span of control states that administrative efficiency is increased by limiting the span of control of a leader to no more than five or six subordinates whose work interlocks."[14]

In his research Lawrence conceived of a formal organization "as a social system that is formed to serve certain purposes, and to which individuals and small groups act as contributors. Each organization exists in an environment that determines certain required behavior that the organization must perform if it is to survive. Each organization, with its required behavior as a starting point, evolves behavioral characteristics that are unique to it and tend to persist over time in certain patterns. . . .

"Any organization to achieve its purpose must have a set of activities designed to perform its purpose—it must have a production system. . . . Our organization must also have a set of interactions that serves to bind the required activities together—it must have a communication-decision system. Such a system would ideally function to provide each person in the organization with all the available information that could help him perform his assigned activities. It would also function so that the necessary choices or decisions between alternate actions would be made for the organization by one who was most expert on the issue involved, regardless of his title or position. . . . This model of a communication system could not properly be labeled either a centralized or decentralized system but simply a functional system. . . . We need a set of sentiments that would function to ensure the full contribution of those working in the organization. Ideally we would want one sentiment to be dominant in all employees from top to bottom, namely, a complete loyalty to the organizational purpose."[15]

In addition to understanding the formal organization it is necessary for administrative leaders to understand the informal organization of their agency. Various authorities have described informal organization in similar terms. Brannen indicates that informal organization is a natural outgrowth of formal organization when he observes, "Most formal organizational structures are comprised of smaller groups of employees who are in frequent contact with one another. Each individual will have frequent contacts with a relatively small number of people. These individuals often form identifiable groups. Their relations become standardized patterns of acceptable behavior: Each person knows what is expected of him and what he can expect of others. These groups make effective technical co-operation possible. They increase stability, provide channels of communication, and routinize many relations. Individuals derive satisfaction and a sense of security from identifying themselves as groups of this informal type. In addition, these groups have leadership positions that will be filled by one employee or another. They have certain relations with other groups, supervisors, and with the organization as a whole. The pattern of relationships and the hierarchy of status positions that grow out of these natural groupings of people are called the informal organization. The informal organization influences the perception of the members of a formal organization. We are all influenced by social pressures. We try to meet the expectations of people with whom we are in frequent contact. We want their good will. As members of various groups and social organizations, we encounter group values, attitudes, and sentiments that determine what is expected of the members of the group. We are subjected to considerable social pressure to conform to the group concept of acceptable behavior."[16]

Dubin observes, "The informal group is something we distinguish from the formal organization. It is a smaller grouping of people and may function either to subvert the purposes of the larger structure or to support them. It is a spontaneous group that arises simply because men associate with one another. Such informal groups are to be found in all kinds of organizations."[17]

Preiss points out that "An informal organization is one which is not officially sanctioned by, or included in, any given chart or blueprint which explains formal organizational relations. It is, so to speak, not acknowledged to be essential or contributory to the successful operation of formal organization. This lack of recognition is not by any means a denial of existence but is rather a denial of legitimacy. One may be well aware of these outside groups yet not include them in the hierarchy of sanctioned positions and relationships. Informal organizations lack legitimacy and recognition in the formal organization, they are small and exist largely by way of face-to-face relationships, they have a structure and a system of norms and values to regulate internal behavior, they have members who experience a sense of belonging or of group identity, often their members have antecedence and relationships which reflect reference groups outside of the formal organization. . . . Informal organization seems to focus around

1. Occupational interests, that is, horizontal rather than vertical.

2. Social recreational interests emphasizing non-job activities.

3. Past history and experience such as previous employment, mutual friends, coming from the same town or state or physical similarity.

4. Personal attraction. . . .

Actually, the informal organization may be helpful in terms of the formal organization.

1. It may help to preserve the formal system by compensating for defects and weaknesses within it.

2. The informal organization may help to assess weaknesses in the formal organization and call attention to new needs and requirements.

3. The informal organization often provides outlets for tension and stresses that occur.

4. Informal groups often become change agents and may serve as the interaction framework where plans and programs for change have been developed and discussed. On the other hand, informal groups may disrupt the formal

system and may be incompatible as to purposes and may increase the tension and stresses and may act as a hindrance to change."[18]

Stone likewise sees the informal organization as being extremely influential in terms of behavior. He says, "In the spontaneous daily contacts that take place between individuals, loyalties and social patterns of conduct are developed that result in cohesive group patterns. Where intimacy and freedom of expression develop, motives that seem otherwise inappropriate have meaning for the work situation. It is at this level of informal organization where redirection and utilization of motives is most evident; and it is at this level usually where the strongest resistance to change occurs. At the level of informal organization, actions of individuals can and do create changes in social behavior that seem little short of miraculous."[19]

What are some of the spontaneous daily contacts in the agency? Among those that could be listed are the coffee break time, the luncheon period, the period when persons are going to and from work together, the casual conversation in the corridor and in the rest rooms and of course the before and after meetings get togethers which are a common phenomenon of most groups.

Doutt stresses the fact that administrative leaders must not only be aware of informal organization but must endeavor to influence these informal groups. He says that these informal personal relationships among workers themselves provide group members with " (1) a feeling of integrity and dignity and a sense of belonging, (2) authority to reject or accept new ideas, (3) a vehicle for communication, (4) a meaning for the day, (5) the enforcement of codes of conduct. . . . The task of management is to create a permissive atmosphere in which informal groups may jell and come to fruition."[20]

Interaction

The individual and his associates are constantly interacting with each other. As the administrator seeks to understand the individual in relation to his fellow workers he naturally surveys the interaction process. Some of the questions administrative leaders might well ask are: How does the individual effect interaction? What does it mean when an individual cannot participate or interact with others? What does it mean when interaction is always leader-focused rather than group member-focused? What significant changes in interaction should we look for in judging group progress?

Some of the findings regarding the process of interaction that may be helpful to administrative leaders are:

First, the amount of interaction increases with the increase in the cohesiveness of the task group.

Second, in addition to speech or verbalizations around the issue being discussed interaction includes facial expressions, gestures, bodily attitudes, emotional signs, or nonverbal acts of various kinds, either expressive and nonfocal, or more definitely directed toward other people.

Third, every problem-solving group must deal with the factors of cognitive orientation, *what is it we are talking about?;* affective orientation, *how does it affect us?;* and conative orientation, *what shall we do about it?*

Fourth, over a period of time the distribution of interaction will change as the security of group members increases.

Fifth, if the interactions between the members of the group are frequent, sentiments of liking will grow up between them and these sentiments will lead in turn to further interactions.

Sixth, the more secure the person, the more comfortable he is, the wider will be his range of interactions.

Seventh, changes in the outer situations surrounding the task group will make for change in the amount, distribution, and direction of interaction within the group.

Eighth, insecure persons may tend to interact with persons of higher social rank or greater authority.

Ninth, the emotional component in interaction is the dynamic force which makes for individual change.

The administrator is always responsible for recommending and developing a framework within which the interactions of people can occur with a focus on the goals of the agency.

Structure

A structure is customarily defined as a framework or support for an enterprise. It should be noted, in addition, that structure is itself a means or network of channels and relationships through which individuals and groups are enabled to work together effectively. Structure refers primarily to the channels through which the services of the agency are determined, planned, and made available to people. Organization is the act or process of bringing together or arranging the related groups of the agency into a working whole.

In the creation of a suitable structure for a community service agency many factors must be taken into account. The legal basis for the agency, as well as its functional area of service, are factors. The size of the agency and the size of the community have a bearing on decisions regarding structure and organization. The place of the constituency or members varies among the agencies and will call for special consideration. Agencies which are building-centered will need a structure different from those that are program or neighborhood centered. The structure of a multiple-function agency will be more complex than that of a single-function agency. Agencies which have many volunteer workers or which have central headquarters and several district or branch offices will have to consider these factors in the creating and maintaining of a workable structure.

Many organizations are hierarchies in a structural sense. The dictionary describes the hierarchy as "a body of officials disposed organically in ranks and orders each subordinate to the one above it." The hierarchy as a form of structure can best be pictured as a pyramid. In the true hierarchy there are clearly established top-down authority relationships. There are relatively rigid levels of job responsibility and status with the chief executive on the top level, below him sub-executives and supervisors, below them staff workers, below them clients, or persons served. The more sharply the status hierarchy is defined, the more difficult it is to advance. In the hierarchy there are formal channels of communication from the top to the bottom and from the bottom to the top. There is less provision as such for lateral communication. While the hierarchical form of organization is satisfactory for certain kinds of enterprises the hierarchy is not a satisfactory form of organization for the community service agency. In the community service agency the organizational form must provide for the growth of co-operative relationships, and free-flowing cross-communication must be fostered.

Organization Principles

When the administrator thinks about the organization of his agency he will be helped if he reviews some of the often-stated principles of organization. He should begin by listing all of the necessary things to be done for the achievement of the purposes of the agency. Next, he should spell out and define and assign the tasks and responsibilities to the various individuals or groups within the agency that are available to carry forward its work. He will then group the closely related tasks into a logical design and in so doing he will attempt to avoid duplication, overlapping, and repetition of work. As he groups the tasks, he will create a structure with the smallest number of units possible and with as few levels as possible. As he looks again at the work to be done he will endeavor to determine whether or not tasks are equitably distributed and whether or not the appropriate group or individual has been assigned the task. Along with this he will be conscious of the need to provide for a system of reviewing work accomplishments, modifying and adapting the work assignments and in addition he will provide for the necessary training and retraining of individuals and work groups.

Criteria of adequacy for agency structure and organization include the following points:

First, the structure should be no more extensive than is needed to support properly the work of the agency. Every effort should be made to keep structure at a minimum, with simplicity rather than complexity as an objective.

Second, a good structure is economical to manage from a time, money, and leadership standpoint.

Third, when structure is well constituted there is an orderly flow of work through the agency; there is uniformity of procedure, and a regularity of service.

Fourth, adequate structure clarifies the areas of responsibility for individuals and groups so that they know what they are to do and how their work relates to the work of others.

Fifth, good structure shows the relation of the agency to the community and the other agencies with which it may be working. If various levels of government are involved or national-local affiliations are present these likewise are shown.

Sixth, satisfactory structure provides for an orderly grouping of the various duties which must be performed and enables specialized tasks to be departmentalized.

Seventh, adequate structure brings about two-way communication, both vertical and horizontal, and tends to stimulate interaction.

Eighth, when structure is indigenous to the agency which it serves it creates unity rather than separation and helps to bring about real co-ordination and integration.

Administrative leaders must work at creating unity in many ways, recognizing that it may be difficult. One executive used the staff meeting to face the problem: "At a meeting of the professional and the clerical staffs we discussed the tendency to speak of what *you* do and what *we* do. It is hard to see and work for the agency as a whole. Talking it over seems to help staff think in terms of the total organization and points up opportunities to build unity."

Ninth, to be adequate for the modern community service agency, structure must call for broad participation in policy making on the part of the many groups that make up the agency. This means there is a reasonably rapid transmittal of information up and down and across the agency as well as a minimum of isolation between levels.

Tenth, flexibility is a criterion of structure, along with periodic review and evaluation.[21]

A good structure helps to create morale and work satisfaction. In a very real sense agency structure must grow and develop out of process and must be considered equally dynamic with purpose and program. As was pointed out in a recent conference, "Structure is effective when it evolves from program, when it serves to integrate decentralized program into the agency as a whole, when it provides channels of communication between parts of the whole and when it allows program to develop and progress."[22] It must be remembered that every agency is made up of a number of parts. Organization is basically a matter of arranging activity among these parts. Complex agencies provide greater opportunities for membership participation in the actual day-to-day planning and operation of the service. Structure must always be thought of as a means to an end, but it is in addition a way of providing opportunities for personal growth and development, which is one of the major goals of many organizations. Uniformity in the structure and organization is not desirable; in fact, it is not possible because communities differ and agencies differ also.

The Metropolitan Agency

Today, many agencies are metropolitan in scope and have a central or headquarters unit and a number of branches or geographically dispersed local offices where services are rendered in various neighborhoods. As one contrasts these large metropolitan agencies with the small community agency it is important to observe that many more people are involved in leadership capacities and there is likely to be a significant turnover of people in these leadership jobs. In addition, the metropolitan agency covers a far wider geographic territory. Usually several communities and neighborhoods are involved; thus there is a wide range of cultural variation. The metropolitan agency is more complex from the standpoint of services expected and programs offered. Because of this it is more difficult to integrate and create a unified agency. Furthermore an examination of the organizational charts of these large agencies points out the fact that there are many more task groups involved in the administrative process. Thus, there is a far more complicated structure and there seems to be an obvious heavy emphasis on the representative group rather than the direct face-to-face participation on the part of all of the members or the people served.

As one visualizes the metropolitan agency at work there can be considerable geographic, social, and emotional distance from the center of the agency to the periphery where services are rendered. Communication lines are much longer and the communication problems are more noticeable. Furthermore, the metropolitan agency is required to decentralize more of its authority and responsibility out to the people; thus new kinds of leadership training and new kinds of skills must be developed. Some would suggest that the major problem of the metropolitan agency is that of allocating authority to the local offices or divisions. It should be observed also that the metropolitan agency has greater interlocking relationships with other community agencies, because large metropolitan areas have more federation and more planning and a more complicated community agency structure. The metropolitan agency has far greater capital investments and far greater financial operations. This requires more in the way of organization and system than is true in the small agency. It is true, also, that the dynamics of change are more and more complicated in the large agency, and it is true that leadership responsibilities are considerably heavier for certain persons.

A number of problems of administration seem to grow out of the unique aspects of the metropolitan agency. First among the problems is the inevitable confusion regarding the nature of the democratic process and the fact that in the large situation there must be modifications in this process. It is clearly different but it is no less democratic. A second problem is that of professional and volunteer roles, relationships, responsibility, and authority. This, too, is not surprising, because the situation itself is the producer of an increasingly complex series of operations. The third problem is that of individual responsibility and group responsibility for work assignments. A fourth area of concern is that of providing a structure or an organization of the various working groups, all of which must have defined responsibilities. Then there is the problem of membership involvement, which is clearly more difficult when there are more members and when they are more widely scattered and when they represent far greater variations as individuals. The sixth problem is the problem of communication when lines are long, and delegation when many people must do parts of jobs, and representation when many decisions have to be made by representative groups. A seventh problem is that of interagency relationships because they are time consuming, because they are required, because they are essential and tend to represent a basic community pattern of work. The eighth problem is the need to spell out a different kind of role for administrative leaders who occupy these important posts in the metropolitan agencies.

In discussing the role of the administrator in large decentralized organizations Smith makes the point that "The chief executive . . . must be able to 'live' with both conflict and uncertainty—for the more layers of officers he has, the more disagreements he will have to iron out both when planning organization change and when conducting routine operations. The greater the number of levels under him, and the more widely scattered they are, the less certain he can be about who actually does what and how well. . . . He must know intimately the key men in key jobs and give all members of this group a clear picture of individual responsibilities and group relationships. . . . His own behavior must be consistent with his pronouncements. . . . He must maintain free and adequate communication both vertical and horizontal. . . . He must allow subordinates to do some things less well than he himself could do them—he must accept the mistakes as a part of the cost of letting men grow, or of letting local organizations become strong and more nearly self-sufficient. . . . He must continually assess the value to the organization of contributions made by key executives. . . . In some, the chief executive is the one who must see that the organization plan is sound in its basic assumptions, that it is run by capable people, that it works. He must see that the company responds to the challenge of change. He must be willing to examine it honestly and try to determine whether the fault lies in the concepts of the plan itself, in the abilities of key people, or in his own method of administration."[23]

Some authorities have accented the fact that the larger the organization the smaller the proportion of members who can really participate in the major decisions and the larger the proportion of people who must merely carry out policies which are set higher up. This position is disputed by Cleveland, who says:

"A large organization has so many more important decisions to be made that there is proportionately more, not less, decision-making authority to go around. The larger the organization and the wider its reach, the more lateral contacts it has to make and maintain, the more complexities must be sorted out by experts on complexity— which is to say leaders. . . . The complexity of modern society and the omnipresence of large organizations not only provide an opportunity for the fullest development of the responsible self; they actually place a premium on the exercise of a greater measure of personal responsibility by more people than ever before. . . . This increase in the extent to which each individual is personally responsible to others is most noticeable in a large bureaucracy. No one person 'decides' anything; each 'decision' of any importance is the product of an intricate process of brokerage involving individuals inside and outside the organization who feel some reason to be affected by the decision, or who have special knowledge to contribute to it. The more varied the organization's constituency, the more its decisions affect 'the public,' the more outside 'veto groups' will need to be taken into account. But, even if no outside consultations were involved, sheer size would produce a complex process of decision. For a large organization is a deliberately created system of tensions into which each individual is expected to bring work ways, viewpoints, and outside relationships markedly different from those of his colleagues. It is the administrator's task to draw from these disparate forces the elements of wise action from day to day, consistent with the purposes of the organization as a whole."[24]

As one thinks about the complexities of large organizations two fundamental aspects are apparent. In the first place, there must be a considerable decentralization of authority; and in the second place, there must be the development of an informal organization out on the periphery away from central authority in order to relate people to the organization. As has been pointed out, "One of the important positive functions of this decentralization of authority is that those who are responsible for making decisions about the primary tasks are the ones most likely to have the greatest amount of substantive knowledge upon which to base their decisions because of the close contact they have with these tasks. On the other hand, the decentralization operates to promote intimate contacts and this in turn leads to the development of informal organization."[25]

The larger the organization the greater the need for integrative leadership. As Dimock puts it, "All large-scale organizations need strong, constructive, imaginative leadership to pull together all the elements of the program which otherwise tend to fly apart. . . . The larger the body . . . the greater is the likelihood that the parts will be separated from the whole; that segmentation will drain the program's energies and halt enterprise. It is integrative leadership that keeps the parts together, and hence leadership is more ncessary in large . . . institutions than it is in smaller, more informal ones. . . . There must be some one person at the top to watch over the program so as to keep it together, to keep it responsible, to combat self-centeredness, to promote innovation and vitality. And there must be extension of leadership on subordinate levels so as to form a kind of network through which the influence of the top man is carried thorughout the organization."[26]

Characteristics of Effective Organizations

Administrative leaders must work out a philosophy of human organization and must be aware of the conditions and characteristics of effectiveness. They should have a growing conception of what must be provided in the agency setting if it is to be thought of as being well organized and effective in carrying forward its work.

As observed by a student of educational administration, "Studies of effective social institutions indicate certain essential characteristics. Each of the members has a clear perception of his role and of his status in the organization. The perceptions of their several roles by various members of the organization are reasonably congruent. When the institution is composed of individuals with different abilities and functions and when their effectiveness depends largely upon their own exercise of initiative, originality, and judgment, the leadership of the institution depends less on rules and directives for achieving some unity and much more on the development of the members' shared values and purposes. Furthermore, an effective institution provides rewards for competent performance of roles and it provides a system of learning which re-enforces the acquisition of more effective behavior patterns by the members. It has a two-way communication system which provides for the development and formulation of policies and directives and also for the feedback which helps the individuals to judge the effects of their efforts and to be guided thereby."[27]

Bennis accents the fact that "All organization should be geared to effectiveness—that is achieving organizational goals (production), efficiency—creation of an interpersonal work system which would facilitate the output goals toward (worker relationships). The optimum organization is one where effectiveness and efficiency are maximized, where workers' needs and organizational needs are satisfied to the greatest extent—This new orientation to administration entails (1) wide participation in decision making rather than centralized decision making, (2) recognition of the face-to-face group, rather than the individual, as the basic unit of organization, (3) mutual confidence, rather than authority, as the integrative force in organization, (4) responsibility of the supervisor as the agent for maintaining intragroup communication rather than as the agent of higher authority, (5) growth of members of the organization to greater responsibility, rather than external control of the members' performance of their tasks."[28]

As Tead has observed, "The purposes, goals, aims of a given institution must be at once clear, convincing, justifiable and persuasively invoked by administrators in relation to every last soul in the organization. . . . The stronger the purposiveness which can come to motivate the largest possible numbers in the associated groups, the smoother and the more efficacious are likely to become the labors required to do the job."[29]

Agency administrative leaders should remember that their organizations are always dynamic rather than static. They are in flux; they are alive; they do not stand still. It should be remembered that no two agencies are exactly alike and that many variables are always operating. In addition, it should be remembered that people view the agency differently. They have different degrees of interest in it and identification with it. They have different degrees of commitment to it, and this commitment may grow and strengthen or may diminish. Furthermore, agencies have certain mood swings when they are at a high point of growth and accomplishment and other mood periods when progress is less direct and less noticeable. In addition, agencies as human organizations have change processes which in themselves represent the underlying dynamics of growth. The image of the agency in the community is of great importance. How it is regarded in the minds of the members, the users, and other participants is a matter of major concern. In the next chapter community factors and forces will be reviewed.

NOTES

1. Crawford H. Greenwalt, *The Uncommon Man* (New York, N.Y.: McGraw-Hill Book Co., 1959), pp. 25–27.

2. Robert Dubin, *Human Relations in Administration* (New York, N.Y.: Prentice-Hall, 1951), p. 384.

3. Harleigh B. Trecker, *Group Process in Administration* (revised and enlarged; New York, N.Y.: The Woman's Press, 1950), pp. 16–17. Out of print.

4. Wallace Sayre, "Some General Observations on the Principles of Administration." Presented at Conference of Association of University Programs in Hospital Administration, Lake Shore Club, Chicago, Ill., December 27–30, 1954.

5. Harvey Schoenfeld, "Interrelationships in the Hospital," *Hospital Administration*, Spring, 1959.

6. William Caudill, *The Psychiatric Hospital as a Small Society* (Cambridge, Mass.: Harvard University Press, 1958), p. 3.

7. Leonard R. Sayles, "Work Group Behavior and the Larger Organization," in Conrad M. Arensberg (ed.), *Research in Industrial Human Relations* (New York, N.Y.: Harper & Brothers, 1957), p. 131.

8. Elton Mayo, *The Social Problems of an Industrial Civilization* (Boston, Mass.: Harvard University Graduate School of Business Administration, Division of Research, 1945), p. 111.

9. Chris Argyris, *Personality and Organization* (New York, N.Y.: Harper & Brothers, 1957), p. 53.

10. Warren G. Bennis, "Problem-Oriented Administration," *Hospital Administration*, Winter, 1960.

11. Gordon R. Clapp, "The Social Scientist and the Administrative Art" in Leonard D. White (ed.), *The State of the Social Sciences* (Chicago, Ill.: University of Chicago Press, 1956), p. 395.

12. Charles E. Redfield, *Communication in Management* (Chicago, Ill.: University of Chicago Press, 1953), pp. 11, 9–10.

13. Chris Argyris, "Personality and Organization," *Hospital Administration*, Winter, 1960, p. 15.

14. Chris Argyris, *Personality and Organization* (*op. cit.*), pp. 59–64.

15. Paul R. Lawrence, *The Changing of Organizational Behavior Patterns—A Case Study of Decentralization* (Boston, Mass.: Harvard University Graduate School of Business Administration, Division of Research, 1958), pp. 6, 207–208.

16. Ted R. Brannen, "The Organization as a Social System," *Hospital Administration*, Spring, 1959.

17. Robert Dubin, *op. cit.*, p. 57.

18. Jack Preiss, "The Phenomenon of Informal Organization," *Hospital Administration*, Spring, 1959.

19. Robert C. Stone, "The Social Context of Motivation," *Hospital Administration*, Winter, 1960.

20. John T. Doutt, "Management Must Manage the Informal Group Too," *Advanced Management*, May, 1959.

21. Harleigh B. Trecker, *op. cit.*, pp. 41–43.

22. Report of *Workshop on Expansion and Decentralization of YWCA Program*, Arden House, Harriman, N.Y. January 12–15, 1959 (New York, N.Y.: Eastern Region, Community Division, National Board, YWCA).

23. George Albert Smith, Jr., *Managing Geographically Decentralized Companies* (Boston, Mass.: Division of Research, Graduate School of Business Administration, Harvard University, 1958), pp. 85–86.

24. Harlan Cleveland, "Dinosaurs and Personal Freedom," *Saturday Review*, February 28, 1959.

25. Oscar Grusky, "Role Conflict in Organization," *Administrative Science Quarterly*, March, 1959.

26. Marshall Dimock, *Administrative Vitality* (New York, N.Y.: Harper & Brothers, 1959), p. 175.

27. Ralph W. Tyler, "Insight from the Behavioral Sciences," in *Faculty-Administration Relationships* (Washington, D.C.: American Council on Education, May, 1957).

28. Warren G. Bennis, *op. cit.*

29. Ordway Tead, "Reflections on the Art of Administration," *Hospital Administration*, Winter, 1959, pp. 9–10.

CHAPTER 4

Understanding the Community

Social AGENCIES are inevitably affected by community factors and forces. It is impossible to think of administration in terms of internal organization alone because every agency operates as a part of a community. The effective administrator must understand the community and must establish and maintain strong community relations. Most social institutions today whether they represent business, industry, education, or community service are spending more time and thought on understanding their place in the community and working effectively within it.

Importance of Community Understanding

There are many reasons why administrators must understand the community where their agency is located.

First, only through studying and knowing the community can they know what the needs of the people are. Knowledge of community needs makes it possible for the agency to define its role and the services it will offer in trying to meet these needs. Thus the community is a major source of need determination. Spencer emphasizes this when she says, "The locus of the agency is the community and everything which the agency does should be focused on community needs and directed toward the intermeshing of its program with other agency programs to provide optimum service on a community-wide basis. Although services have grown up agency by agency, and each has the legal right to raise its own funds and carry out its activities autonomously within certain broad legal limits everything indicates that the community should exercise the controlling function in terms of the community good. The problem is whether or not we build into the agency administrative process on the part of every participant—board, staff and clientele—an awareness of community needs so that agency behavior can be patterned accordingly. When this is achieved voluntarily, as a part of agency administration, rather than through dictation from a community-wide or governmental body, and when it is achieved by the majority of agencies in any community, the result should be agency administration at a high level; it also should make possible the best type of community planning and co-ordination."[1]

Second, the community is also a major factor in resource provision. Out of the community must come leadership, finances, broad understanding and support, and the climate or atmosphere within which work can be carried on successfully.

Third, how the agency is regarded in the community, its standing, the extent to which it is understood, is of the utmost importance. The agency administrative team must pay great attention to the "image" of the agency as it is seen by the community. This is realized by an executive when she writes:

"The executive and president have tried to assess the strength and weakness of this agency and its position in the community. The executive had positive ideas, especially on program, finance, and leadership, which she explained to the president, who agreed in some cases and suggested certain changes in others. The objective approach of the executive was invaluable; she studied the agency and tested her ideas on others, notably some of the staff on the Chest and Council. Her judgments were modified at points, confirmed at others."

Members of the board and the major administrative committees have helped develop these assessments to the point where they furnish the background for major actions. As the executive says, "Assessment and action are interlocking, and one must check assessments repeatedly."

Fourth, today community service agencies cannot operate alone; they are inevitably a part of community planning and federated financing. Thus, agencies must work with one another within the regular community planning channel.

Fifth, today there is much more co-operative or interagency work in most communities. This means that administrative leadership must understand the principles of co-operation and must know what is involved.

Sixth, the community is changing very rapidly. This means that agencies must adapt to social changes and must plan ahead so that new purposes and new programs will be available to meet changing conditions.

The push of population to the suburbs has brought about new demands for services, as is illustrated by this comment from an executive:

"Because of the increased development of the community into outlying areas, we are having many requests for program in these areas. In a good many cases, we have been able to offer new program, chiefly that for young mothers; in these areas, we are conscious of the fact that with all the requests for services that are coming to us, we need to be very much alert to analyzing all of these possibilities in the light of our purpose."

The impact of intercultural factors is emphasized in this excerpt from a community description:

"This is a fascinating area with many racial, cultural and religious groupings—predominating are Yugoslavs, Italians, Mexicans, Scandinavians, Negroes, Japanese, Philippinos, and sprinklings of many others. A large part of the nationality groupings listed for the total population of the city are concentrated in our area. In fact, in one year a Branch Post Office said mail to every Post Office in the world had cleared through it. Although our area has such a cosmopolitan population there are some neighborhoods where the population is very homogeneous. In fact, it tends to become segregated in new suburban developments."

Another executive lists the following conditions and forces which effect the work of her agency:

"The changing role of women
   Early marriage age—families completed earlier
   Employment patterns
Limited adult education opportunities
Conservative religious community
   Many groups against such activities as dancing, card
      playing
Limited public recreation facilities and program
Divisive character of textile area and larger community
Over-organization of women into all kinds of groups
Growing complexity of the community
Highly organized structure of teen-age life
   Extracurricular activities
   Sororities and fraternities in some high schools
   Active and full church programs
Women involved in strong, well-organized, and active
   church life
Geographical expansion of city
Lack of community programs for 'aging' (35 and up)
Change in population make-up
   More younger people
   More older people"

Thus during the past two decades a considerable number
of major changes have taken place in the community. Consider, for example, the growth of large metropolitan areas
with usually a declining population in the central city and
a rapidly growing population in the suburban areas. Consider, also, the hundreds of urban renewal and redevelopment projects that are under way in the country today.
Furthermore, consideration must be given to the multiple-

level involvement of government in all forms of community service. In addition there have been many changes in governmental agencies in terms of authority, scope, and size.

But it is not always easy to discuss community change, as evidenced by this candid quotation: "How difficult it is to discuss objectively something that might involve making a change. It almost seems that the more we are surrounded by changing situations the more tenaciously we cling to the known and familiar. In our rapidly changing community, we go to town in the morning, and when we return at night whole buildings are gone. We brag about the fast-growing area, the numbers of people moving in, and at the same time resist them. Our comfortable way of life is threatened. We have certain vested interests to protect, such as buildings and organizational structure."

In a brilliant paper prepared by the staff of the National Federation of Settlements and Neighborhood Centers[2] six major areas of community change are highlighted which have profound implications for program and services. The list includes changing population patterns, changing city structure, changing educational patterns, changing patterns of leisure, changing patterns of employment, and changes in family life.

What Must Be Understood about the Community

Administrative leaders must know the people and the institutions of the community. They must know the variety and quality of resources that exist in the community for meeting the needs of people. They must know as much as possible about the social situations that have contributed to and are contributing to the experience of the people they are serving. In addition, they must be able to define the agency's geographic community and, at the same time, endeavor to understand the make-up, the behavior, and the attitudes of the different local communities or neighborhoods within their service area. Furthermore, they should understand the interdependence of people, institutions, and the community. They must know community resources in terms of leadership and financial potential.

An administrator highlights the importance of understanding the community in the following excerpt from a report:

"Since 1945 the population has become more diverse. The permanent location of the Air Force Base and the widespread diversification of industry, with many new industries, have brought into the community many new citizens from throughout the country, and indeed from other countries of the world.

"So great has been the geographical expansion also, that the entire county can more nearly be called the community unit now. There have been a number of shopping centers established contiguous to the various residential areas.

"The change is further reflected in the expansion of industry throughout the county into formerly predominantly agricultural areas.

"The metropolitan area now includes about 125,000 persons against about 90,000 ten years ago.

"Because of the enormous growth and change, few of the community facilities or programs are adequate. Schools are overflowing, some on two-shift schedules; traffic problems are paramount. An additional water system is being constructed and the water and sewer systems are soon to be studied; social welfare programs are housed in old and inadequate buildings; there is no public recreation program outside city proper area, and it is even limited there; no plan exists for recreation for the county; programs are impeded by conflict in jurisdiction between city and county units of government."

In a much larger community some of the same factors are present:

"The agency services a tri-county area which includes thirty-eight cities and villages. The 4,000,000 population, approximately half of which is in the city proper, is a typical melting pot mixture; the major nationality groups are Canadian, Polish, Italian, German, English, Scotch and Hungarian. Negroes account for 22 per cent of the population of the city and 5 per cent of the population of the surrounding areas. The total population of the city has increased 17 per cent since 1960, the surrounding area, 133 per cent, and the Negro population, 100 per cent.

"The pattern of mobility is similar to that of other cities: rural to urban, city to suburbs, relocation due to slum clearance and highway programs, movement of labor force in relation to availability and employment, etc. There has been movement of Negroes from the core of the middle-aged sections of the city, but the pattern of the Negro population occupies many widespread areas so that the geographic areas serviced by the five branches of our agency are integrated with the exception of one, which is exclusively white.

"Protestant, Catholic, and Jewish groups all occupy important roles in the community. There are about thirty-nine synagogues. Surveys indicate that Roman Catholics form one-third to one-half of the population. The religious groups, through their federations, councils, etc., give vital and increasing leadership to social issues such as interracial problems.

"While the area has many diversified industries, it is dominated by heavy manufacturing and industries related thereto. The economy, therefore, quickly reflects the economic vitality of the nation. Unemployment has been a widespread problem the past year. Considerable community tension also arises around contract negotiations or strikes in the heavy industries, since these affect a large part of the population. Union-management relations are of great importance in community co-operation as well as strife, labor playing a vital role in community-wide organizations such as the United Fund and the Hospital Fund.

"In the field of Human Relations, official and private circles have done much constructive thinking and planning. Housing (both low-cost rental and private), job opportunities, police relationships, and hospital and public accommodations are of special concern to the Negro community. There is no significant integration in public housing, and while movement of whites to Suburbia has opened up a tremendous amount of private housing spreading out from the core of the city to Negroes, the historical patterns of segregation have tended to be maintained despite court rulings in recent years. A state-wide F.E.P. law has opened up job opportunities for Negroes."

Geographic Service Area

An effective agency has defined the geographic area within which it will work and render service. It endeavors to understand basic social, physical, and cultural facts about the area and to use such information in planning its work. This means that administrative leaders must make sure that the agency has collected factual data on the geographic area it serves. Also, administrative leaders must make use of such community facts as population, occupation, income, housing, and the like in program planning. Beyond this, administrative leaders must make sure that the agency has regular methods and procedures for keeping up-to-date with community fact gathering. Usually, it is helpful if the agency has a committee on community study and community needs. In addition, the agency must be familiar with the work of similar and allied agencies and must study major trends in community life in order to anticipate or forecast major changes which will call for modification of agency program.

Maps are used to good advantage to help an agency program committee understand the community: "We used maps of city planning and types of housing. The former showed zoning and pointed out quite plainly a lack of public park facilities in our area as well as a tremendous transition. It was interesting to be able to see zoning and housing together. Committee members seemed more responsive and interested during this meeting than before and had more suggestions and questions."

Factual data about the community were brought to the

attention of planning committees: "We summarized all of the information on housing, economic and population trends, available program, and degree of participation. By doing this for the total area we hoped to encourage the group to use factual material and understand its implications in arriving at conclusions as to what our program should be."

Understanding Persons Served

An effective agency has made decisions regarding the clientele it will endeavor to work with. It seeks to understand the people with whom it works and it endeavors to help these people become related to the agency as a whole. This means that the agency has a written definition specifying the clientele it will serve in terms of age, sex, program services, and the like. This definition is publicized and known by the community. The agency has a systematic method of collecting social, cultural, and general background data about the people it serves, and it uses these data in planning services for them. The effective agency has written policies and procedures regarding how people may use, join, or participate in the agency. It keeps statistical records on the people it serves and with whom it works. It has identifying information on each individual or family with whom it works. It uses this information in program planning. Furthermore, the agency has a planned procedure for admission, reception, or intake of new clientele designed to help persons understand the agency and the agency to understand the persons who are coming to it. The agency makes regular studies of changes and turnover in the clientele it serves.

In a southern state an executive notes the impact of industry on the lives of people:

"Textile and allied plants make up the major portion of industry. Originally the textile industry was centered in about twenty plants, in a semicircle just outside the city proper. This resulted in sharply defined communities and divisions between the mill area and the remainder of the metropolitan area. Well-organized community life, centering in schools and churches in each mill village and drawn together in a centralized high school for the industrial area, served to keep this section apart, with citizens taking little part in the life of the larger area.

"Also the character of the people contributed to the divisiveness. Having come primarily from the mountain and rural areas, these citizens of Anglo-Saxon stock are proud and strongly individualistic.

"The separateness of this area is still a fact though this too is changing due to more mobility of the population, to the incorporation of the school in the county system of education, to the sale of homes by the mills and the fact that many people now commute to the mills to work rather than living in the village itself."

Co-operation with Other Agencies

As pointed out at a recent YWCA Workshop, "Co-operation with other agencies and community groups is a major means for the YWCA to do its work. Though the YWCA has historically stood for joint undertakings, co-operation now takes on new dimensions and new problems. There is no virtue in co-operating for the sake of co-operation; it is essential only when it helps the YWCA to carry out its purpose. Co-operation is essential because we operate in the midst of all kinds of community forces, groups, and other agencies to which we must relate ourselves. We must participate in community planning with other agencies in order to see clearly the community as a whole, its needs, and our relationship to it. Without co-operation with other agencies it is difficult to get essential facts and to see and plan ahead. We also need to co-operate in order to influence developments and to participate in united action in behalf of a common objective."[3]

When an agency decides to enter into a joint program or a co-operative effort with another agency or several agencies, administrative leaders are responsible for a number of important things. *First,* they should get the facts as to the needs to be met by the co-operative program and should clearly evaluate the resources that are available. *Two,* they should help the Board and other groups see the role of their agency quite clearly and should enter into specific agreement as to who does what. *Three,* they must naturally make sure that the work will be carried on in keeping with the agreed-upon standards and policies of service. *Four,* they must ascertain in advance that the co-operative or interagency approach will yield a better program. *Five,* they must certainly be in on the planning from the very early stages. *Six,* they must spell out the distinctive contributions that can be made by the agency. *Seven,* they must be able to assign the necessary staff and manpower to do the job. *Eight,* they must agree in advance as to the criteria of evaluation that are to be used during and at the conclusion of the co-operative program.

Central Planning and Federated Financing

Almost all administrators and their key volunteers must work closely with the central planning and federated financing agencies.

As Brueckner points out with reference to youth-serving agencies—and it is relevant for almost all agencies today— "Practically all these agencies have found their way into federations of agencies of their own kind, and especially into a position of interdependence with all major community services. This is mainly expressed by the fact that the community network of social services, of which a community center is a part, has become a technical and financial necessity. Planning for social services and financing these services have become tasks which cannot be effectively solved without a co-operative arrangement."[4]

The complexity and vastness of large-city fund raising is pointed up by this description of an urban center:

"This is a United Fund city, the Salvation Army, Red Cross and Community Chest being among the participating agencies. There is a strong move toward a single organization. At present, the Community Chest comprises 160 agencies and the Welfare Council is composed of 299 agencies, private and public. The Federation of Jewish Charities is a constituent of the Chest; Catholic Charities are not. Federated fund raising is fairly old here, having started in 1928. Of late, the campaigns have not been successful. For several years we have tried to reach $15,500,000.

The closest we have come was last year at $13,800,000. The present campaign is leveling off at slightly over $13,500,000. Estimated needs run to about $16,000,000."

The importance of planning is accented by this comment from an executive:

"Social planners in government, Fund, Chest, Council, church and cultural groups are being listened to more attentively than was true five years ago. There is an increasing trend for agencies to work together on community problems. Planning and working together, with the possibilities it engenders, seems to have captured the imagination of the leaders, and is growing."

The brief excerpts which follow illustrate relationship between agency executives and central planning staff:

"I had a conference with the personnel consultant of the Welfare Council to discuss staff line-up necessary for preparation of the budget prior to submitting it to the Chest. The staff situation is definitely related to our Agency Study and points up some problems which we will be discussing. It is necessary to keep the Welfare Council and the Chest informed as to what is going on in regard to the study so that any recommended changes will not come as a surprise. In fact, it is necessary just to let them know that we are studying our work. The personnel consultant was very interested. He felt that the fact that we are trying to make an intelligent approach to our administration problems is important and helpful. This is the first time that a representative of the Welfare Council has visited our agency in the past ten years. He stayed all afternoon discussing our problems."

By consulting with other professionals an executive can learn much about the community:

"Consulted with the executive secretary of the Group Work Division of the Community Welfare Council to learn more about the community and opportunities for our program. Submitted my report to our program planning committee for consideration.

"Met with the executive secretary of the Community Committee to discuss services required in the urban renewal area. We focused upon the needs of women and girls to discover ways for the agency to serve them."

Experimentation and Demonstration

Many agencies are called upon to undertake experimental or demonstration programs in new communities. When this is the case administrative leaders have a major responsibility to develop policy statements or guide lines to the operation of these demonstration or experimental programs. In a recent report from a national agency[5] a number of important points were suggested.

1. Before it is launched the immediate and long-range purposes of a demonstration should be thoroughly understood, clearly stated, and fully agreed upon by the financial sponsors and those who are to be directly responsible for its direction and administration.

2. It is equally important that the community in which a demonstration is to be established be understood as thoroughly as possible by the sponsoring group and the directors of the demonstration.

3. A broad base of participation established early and made up of influential individuals, appropriate agencies, representatives of the pertinent professions and of various civic groups is essential to a successful demonstration.

4. The physical location of a demonstration project should be carefully selected.

5. Early in the demonstration, agreement should be reached between the sponsors of the demonstration and those who will eventually assume full responsibility for it, as to the allocation and sharing of responsibility, including administration, financing, staffing, estimated duration of the demonstration, and arrangements for evaluating methods and results.

6. A statement of the objectives to be gained in the demonstration, together with a timetable of estimated dates, should be set up early.

7. The withdrawal of the sponsor should be gradual and should follow a general plan worked out in advance and agreed upon by the major participants.

8. Frequent and objective analysis of the conduct of the project with the help of outside experts from time to time is helpful in detecting whether a demonstration is maintaining its effective research qualities or becoming merely an orthodox service for program.

9. Before the start of a demonstration, methods should be devised and agreed upon to ensure the evaluation of results and their interpretation to appropriate groups in the community, including, particularly,

those who must one day accept full responsibility for the program. This means extra help on public relations and public education, and a definite built-in plan for research, with ample advice and guidance from outside sources designed to evaluate the various steps in the development of the program and provide for continuing study and analysis.

Administrative Leadership in Community Study

A striking illustration of administrative leadership in community study is provided by the Community Service Society of New York City in their report, *Searchlight on New York* —a progress report on human welfare in New York City. This magnificent study is reported as "an objective appraisal of the present and prospective welfare needs in New York City having in mind the relation of these needs to the activities of the Community Service Society." For two years an appropriately staffed study committee of the Society endeavored to determine the major social and social welfare needs of New York City in the light of the prevailing social climate. In addition, they projected these needs ten years into the future on the basis of known factors in the social and economic development of the city. Furthermore, they catalogued the social welfare resources of the city to determine in what measures these resources were adequate to meet current and perspective social welfare needs. They assessed the current cost of social welfare services both governmental and voluntary, available to residents of New York and determined the income sources available to finance the social welfare program. They defined and evaluated the part that their agency, the Community Service Society, has played and should play in the social welfare program.

In their summary chapter they say, "This study certainly suggests that the time may be right for a far-reaching change of emphasis in our welfare effort. Thoughtful people will, we believe, agree that today's greatest need is for a more direct assault on the causes that lie behind our more serious welfare problems. To mend social damage after it becomes destructive is extremely costly to society both in monetary and in human terms. Increasing efforts must be made, therefore, to prevent the damage. To this end, it would seem apparent that community attention and support must increasingly be directed toward methods of prevention and rehabilitation. . . . Through established techniques of prevention and rehabilitation, not only can many thousands of distressed people be helped to achieve a better life, but the residual burden of their unresolved need can be lifted from the shoulders of the community."[6]

Evaluation of Administration and the Community

The following questions are designed to test the extent to which the agency's administrative processes are soundly related to the community.

1. To what extent does the agency have up-to-date information and basic social facts about the community for use in policy making and program planning?

2. To what extent does the agency have a method of arriving at an understanding of emerging social needs brought about by community changes? Consider, for

example, the implications of such material as the following, stated by an administrator who is describing the area where a youth-service agency is at work: "It's an area of new homes, vast suburban tracts, many of them very picturesque as they are carved out of the hills. There is much mobility into and within the area and many people travel long distances to employment. The Urban-Redevelopment movement is very strong in the older sections. There are three separate public school systems in the area, as well as many parochial schools. Two Junior Colleges are here. Children are bussed long distances to school in some places. Some are on half-day sessions. There is continuous increase in school population with new schools and additions to old ones always under construction. At the present rate a 55 per cent increase is indicated in school population in the next ten years. A tremendous adult education program is provided. A large Americanization program is conducted both in adult school and high school. Public transportation is very limited. What there is, is to the metropolitan centers and none between areas."

3. To what extent are sound communication lines maintained between the agency and other community organizations?

4. To what extent are board members representative of the community?

5. To what extent does the orientation of new volunteers and staff include orientation to the community and planned participation in the community?

6. To what extent do job analyses include specific itemized reference to the individual's responsibility for community participation and leadership?

7. To what extent does the agency make a conscious effort to see itself as the community sees it?

8. To what extent do staff development and in-service training programs include material on the community?

9. To what extent does the agency work with other agencies in common service projects?

10. To what extent does the agency participate in total community planning and co-ordination?

NOTES

1. Sue Spencer, "The Nature of the Administrative Process in a Social Welfare Agency." Paper given at the Annual Forum, National Conference on Social Welfare, Atlantic City, N.J., June 6, 1960.

2. *Neighborhood Goals in a Rapidly Changing World* (New York, N.Y.: National Federation of Settlements and Neighborhood Centers, 1958).

3. *Report of Workshop for Large Associations,* Detroit, March 21–23, 1956 (New York, N.Y.: Community Division, National Board YWCA, 1956), p. 21.

4. William H. Brueckner, "Volunteers in the Youth Serving Agency," in Nathan E. Cohen (ed.), *The Citizen Volunteer* (New York, N.Y.: Harper & Brothers, 1960), p. 128.

5. *Annual Report,* Association for the Aid of Crippled Children, 1956–57 (New York, N.Y.).

6. *Searchlight on New York: A Progress Report on Human Welfare in New York City* (New York, N.Y.: Community Service Society, 1960), pp. 71–72.

PART TWO

SKILL IN ADMINISTRATION

──────────

CHAPTER **5**

Administrative Leadership

IN THE DISCUSSION of administration offered in Chapter 1 it was observed that many different people carry administrative responsibility and provide administrative leadership for the agency. In many agencies two groups of people may be considered as belonging to the corps of administrative leaders. They are, first, the *professional workers,* and second, *administrative volunteers.*

The professional workers include executive directors, who carry the over-all responsibility for the agency, and sub-executives such as assistant or associate executive directors, who carry responsibilities which have been delegated to them. In addition, program directors, directors of casework, and heads of departments who give leadership to services and program must provide leadership for their assigned areas. The same is true for regional, district, branch, center or unit directors whose duties may be related to a specific geographic territory. Professional workers are employed by the agency. They usually devote full time to their assignment and bring special educational preparation and experience to their tasks. Their work requires a high degree of competence based on professional education in the special area of their service. They are expected to make sound professional judgments and to exhibit professional skill in fulfilling their duties.

Administrative volunteers include agency presidents or board chairmen, vice presidents and other officers, the chairmen of key committees, and board members. These volunteers work without salary and are elected or appointed to the positions they freely assume. They devote only part of their time to these duties. They should have a general interest in the work of the agency and a specific competence and contribution to make to the assignment they have taken. In passing, it should be noted that many agencies have other volunteers usually thought of as *program* or *service* volunteers. While their contribution is a major one in terms of agency services and program ordinarily their administrative responsibilities are less and they are not expected to give leadership to administration.

The first group, namely the *professional workers,* and the second group, namely the *administrative volunteers,* are frequently identified as *staff* and *board*. Both groups are needed and both groups provide administrative leadership in line with defined functions and expectations. The way the two groups work together is of the utmost importance.

The governing board and the administrative volunteers, especially officers and committee chairmen theoretically, constitute representation from the community. Through them the community expresses its wishes with regard to goals, policies, and services. Since the agency is created by the community to meet recognized needs and since the community provides the resources necessary to provide services, it is clearly important that the community be responsible for the agency. The governing board becomes a kind of bridge between the general community and the professional staff. Board and staff together develop the needed services. To do this they divide the work to be done and make assignments to individuals and to committees or task groups. These committees require administrative leadership just as the staff workers themselves require overall guidance and direction.

In certain agencies such as those in the informal education, leisure time, and youth-serving fields, the members served occupy a major place in the authority structure. These members elect the board and determine the broad general goals and policies to be pursued.

In all agencies individuals and groups who are carrying work assignments need administrative leadership. Professional workers, non-professional workers, program and service volunteers, committees, councils, and the member body must have someone to help them achieve focus, direction, and accomplishment in their assigned areas of responsibility.

It is true that agencies are different and that there are variations to be taken into account. A small agency may have only one or two professional workers and a very large number of administrative volunteers. A large agency may have many professional workers, including some highly specialized ones, and a relatively small corps of administrative volunteers. In some agencies administrative volunteers also work as service or program volunteers, and in such situations they must keep their roles straight. There are differences, too, in the number and types of committees agencies have. Some have only a few committees while others create many committees because they feel the need to involve more people so as to broaden the understanding of and support for the agency itself. This will clearly create variations in the ways the agency carries on its work. Another area of difference is in the way the executive director is considered. Some agencies delegate much more to the executive than do others. In some situations the president retains a substantial amount of administrative responsibility. Often because of special competence board members or committee chairmen carry a temporary or even continuing assignment in their realms of particular competence. This alters the role of the executive, or at any rate calls for clarity and understanding as to who is responsible for a given task.

Administrative leaders, whether they be professionals or volunteers, must understand the nature of leadership. They must possess certain general qualifications and must develop their self-awareness and self-discipline. They must be clear on the essential features of the democratic method and conduct themselves accordingly. These topics and others will be reviewed in the material which follows.

Definitions and Patterns of Leadership

The following definitions of leadership highlight certain common denominators. Campbell says, "Leadership may be defined as the contribution of a given individual to group effectiveness, mediated through the direct efforts of others rather than through himself."[1]

Barnard says, "Leadership refers to the quality of the behavior of individuals whereby they guide people or their activities in organized effort."[2]

Mayo emphasizes the fact that social skill is basic to leadership. He says, "Technical skill manifests itself as a capacity to manipulate things in the service of human purposes. Social skill shows itself as a capacity to receive communications from others, to respond to the attitudes and ideas of others in such fashion as to promote congenial participation in a common task."[3]

An educational group defines leadership as "that quality in an individual which enables him to affect the intentions and voluntary actions of another. . . . The best leadership comes out of a contributive pattern which encourages and provides opportunities for a contribution of each individual; decisions are fashioned out of the combined thinking of the group affected. . . . Once decisions have been made on the basis of intelligent interaction of the individuals in the group, then the leaders have the responsibility of implementation, reinterpretation, and administration."[4]

In discussing philosophies of leadership McMurry emphasizes the consultative or participative philosophy.

The leader who operates according to this philosophy "encourages maximum participation by his associates and subordinates in decision making." This leader emphasizes goals and sub-goals; he explains conditions and helps group members to plan and organize the steps to be taken. He outlines the methods to be used to reach the goals. He invites others to participate in developing the methods to be used. He evaluates results in terms of the work-centered objectives appropriate to the total situation. He motivates by stressing his followers' personal goals; the project is "we" rather than "I" oriented. McMurry sees, as the principal merits of the consultative participative leadership approach, these factors: "It makes full use of the creative abilities of subordinates by encouraging contributions from them. It provides subordinates with a better understanding of an insight into problems facing the group as a whole. It ensures adequate guidance and support by the leader. It offers opportunities for ego-gratification through participation. It serves to reduce internal friction by providing outlets for them, keeping frustration at a minimum and giving subordinates an awareness of common goals."[5]

Tead says leadership is "the capacity to get others to do what the leader proposes for them to do because they come to want to do it . . . the best administrative leaders are those who have socially justifiable purposes and who enlist loyalty to them by provocative, creative appeals to those groups involved. This is the essence of democratic leadership in that the effort is consciously being made to achieve the institutional goals while trying simultaneously to assure that these implicated are realizing and actualizing themselves as they labor and through their labor for the corporate good. The development or realization of the personalities of the followers has always to be one half of the dual goal of the leader, the other half being to assure that the institution's purpose is well served by the integrated labors of all."[6]

In the excerpt given below the importance of leadership which sets a tone or atmosphere is accented:

"My evaluation of the meeting is that it was perhaps too stiff and lacked spontaneity. Members have not yet caught the enthusiasm of the leaders. I don't think any individual failed in her agenda assignment, but to me it didn't seem to click. There are several reasons for this. The chairman is inexperienced and needs confidence to draw people out. Often when there has been intensive preliminary planning by a core group it is difficult to transfer its feeling to the larger group. Even with the greatest care this may result in directives rather than suggestions. Members of a special committee must work together to get an *esprit de corps*. Perhaps the presence of too much 'top brass' at the meeting cramped their style."

The Democratic Process

Administrative leaders must understand the essential elements in the democratic process, because these elements have a profound bearing on administration.

First, in a democracy the goals and purposes grow out of the social needs of persons. Community service agencies likewise represent the social needs of persons. Their program objectives and the way these objectives are developed and implemented must rest upon a special way of discovering social needs and relating people to one another so that their needs may be met. The modern community service agency does nothing *for* people. It does a great deal *with* people, and its way of doing whatever it does with people must be a first concern of administrators.

Second, in the democratic process the means and the ends must be compatible. Democracy is not a way of doing certain things but a certain *way of doing everything.* If community service agencies are designed to help achieve democratic goals they must use democratic means in their administration. There is no other choice. If people are to be helped to become responsible citizens they must be given responsibility. If administrative leaders propose to develop within persons their democratic skills and capacities there is no way to work except in the democratic way.

Third, the democratic process is a highly developmental one existing in a changing community scene. The democratic process is never absolutely perfect. The democratic doctrine is not a doctrine of the absolute. It is not a doctrine of perfectionism. It is always a "becoming," a striving for better participation, a striving for better decisions, a striving for constructive use of compromise rather than thoughtless compromise, a striving for new forms of organization, a striving to become more democratic. Oftentimes it is observed that community service agencies are too deliberate; they cannot make up their minds; they must always report back to the board or staff. If the agency is to be administered democratically there must be a considerable amount of time spent in involving people in decision making and there must be close communication between all of the responsible parties.

Fourth, an essential element in the democratic process is the wide involvement of people which engages them in creative and co-operative effort. This is often called the element of participation. In this connection the question arises, Who are the people to participate? Every one? Since everyone in the agency cannot participate in every decision there must be criteria of selection. Upon what problems should there be wide involvement and participation of many people? What is the right problem? In this connection a considerable amount of planning and leadership is required. Orderly and designed participation does not hurt the democratic process; in fact, it enhances the process and makes the achievement of goals easier. Participation is costly, and it is time consuming, but it is known that the product which comes out of thoughtful deliberation under skilled leadership is eminently worth the time and the effort put into it.

Fifth, an essential element in the democratic process is that of conferring and communicating. Those persons in charge of community service agencies do a considerable amount of conferring. The question which needs to be answered by administrative leaders is, are we really communicating? Genuine understanding and genuine consent are the end products of good communication. Communication means to share in common rather than to impart to. There are differences here. Much of the so-called communication is more apt to be imparting to. Certainly the imparting of information is important, but what happens to this imparted material, how it becomes shared in common, is always the heart of the communication problem.

When we make cost analyses we discover that conferring and communicating in administration represents a considerable proportion of the agency's budget and staff time. Conferring and communicating is an expensive way of doing the work of the agency. So this question must be raised: Whom should we bring together, how often should we bring them together, why do we bring them together, what are we conferring about, and is there anything to confer about? In a later chapter the process of communication will be discussed at length.

Sixth, in the democratic process people grow and develop through shared responsibility for decisions and for the consequences of their decisions. There is always a concern on the part of the democratic administrator for not only the doing of the job but also how it is done, and doing it so it will contribute to the growth of persons. The fact is very clear that if administration is to be democratic it must keep in mind these two dimensions. A short way of highlighting it is to say that administrative leaders must get their jobs done but at the same time they care deeply about the persons with whom they work. They are concerned about what happens to the people they are working with. The leadership contribution of the administrator who thinks about it in these terms multiplies gradually if out of each experience of doing he can help other persons to learn how to do the next experience a little better. Every experience in working with people ought to help them to be more ready and more equipped to handle the next opportunity.

Seventh, in the democratic process leadership is enormously important. Some people have strange notions about the democratic method. They overlook the fact that the democratic process requires highly skilled leaders. The democratic work group is not an aimless, leaderless work group. In the community service agency, the leadership concept refers both to the volunteer worker and to the employed worker. A higher and higher degree of skill is needed on the part of both.

Eighth, planning is another basic element of the democratic process. It is a planned process. Some people have trouble with this idea. They must remember that the democratic process is not a haphazard, catch-as-catch-can process. It is an orderly sequence with logical steps. The democratic process is based on considered judgment, planfully brought to bear on problems, consistently focused on objectives. It is true, that the way planning is done is important. Some people feel that it would be better if planning did not take so long. They should be reminded that the more remote the goal and the more complicated the goal, the greater the planning task to arrive at a sound way of reaching that goal. Some of the critics of community service agency administration perhaps fail to understand that the goals of these agencies are very complicated goals. Therefore, the structure and sequence of planning have to be related to what the agency is planning for. Educational planning, planning in the field of social service, and in the broad field of human enterprise is inevitably complicated. It means that administrative leaders must spend more time in the planning process.

Ninth, an essential element of the democratic process is the availability of facts, freely secured, open to all as a basis for independent decision. In a democratic society the sources of information are always kept open. Facts are placed on the table, hard facts as well as the easy ones. In a democratic society facts are sought after continuously. Administrative leaders do not conceal the facts; they bring out the facts so that they can be used in decision making. Administrative leaders must ask themselves what facts are needed? In what form are they needed? How can we communicate them? How can we evaluate them? The democratic health of an agency can be measured by looking at the extent to which it does have basic and genuine freedom of information.

Tenth, another essential element in the democratic process is that of creating new unities out of difference and diversity. In a democratic society these unities are achieved and reachieved through the conscious search for difference of points of view, difference in expression, and freedom to disagree. Democratic administrators do not attempt to stifle difference; they covet the contribution of different points of view. Among the questions which must be asked are: Are we sure that we have discussed the problem long enough to draw out the various differences in viewpoint? At what point do we move toward convergence and the search for agreement? Do we have enough similarity of viewpoint to create the necessary unity for making a decision and for carrying forward our work? Democratic administration requires a high degree of functional correlating—a high degree of co-ordinating and relating people with differences. This function of correlating is extremely important. It is important because in any large social institution there must be a division of labor and there must be specialization. It follows then that there must be an assignment of tasks to be done by many people. It follows likewise that there must be a timing of these tasks and a relating of these tasks. This act of relating or co-ordinating or correlating is assuming increasing importance in all administration.

Eleventh, in the modern democratic process representation through delegation of responsibility, authority, and accountability is increasingly required. Even in very small agencies everyone cannot be in on everything face to face. The larger the agency the more necessary it is that administrative leaders give thought to devising various forms of representation. Since the large organization must necessarily become a representative organization and since representatives will be chosen on the basis of qualifications, administrative leaders are concerned about such questions as what do we delegate, how do we do it, and to whom do we delegate?

Qualities Needed by Administrative Leaders

The administrator needs a fund of factual knowledge, mastery of technique, and analytical ability. Glover and Hower say, "the qualities which to our way of thinking distinguish the administrator are his ability to think and act responsibly, to work co-operatively with others, and to provide others opportunities to work effectively and with satisfaction within the group."[7]

Clark and Teall, in discussing the executive director, say "The purpose of the executive director's job is to give focus to the creative processes by which a YWCA becomes a responsible part of the national world movement and

109

operates with integrity in its own community." They go on to say that the professional worker brings into the situation a faith in people, a liking for them, knowledge of the potentialities of persons and the intent to create the climate for their fulfillment."[8]

In a summary of research on leadership Hall says "The responsibility of the leader (executive, chairman) is not primarily to provide directives but to maintain the evocative situation. Though he may be relatively inconspicuous his role is crucial in keeping the goal in sight, creating a warm and permissive atmosphere for participation, recognizing consensus, helping persons find their parts in co-operative effort. We measure the effectiveness of the new leader not in terms of the leadership he exercises, but in terms of the leadership he evokes; not in terms of his power over others, but in terms of the power he releases in others; not in terms of the goal he sets up and the directions he gives, but in terms of the goals and plans of action persons work out for themselves with his help; not in terms alone of products and projects completed, but in terms of growth in competence, sense of responsibility and in personnel satisfactions among many participants. Under this kind of leadership it is not always clear at any given moment just who is leading, nor is this very important. What is important is that many may learn how to set their teeth in a problem, to apply their minds to it, to work together on it; leadership of this kind gets more done—more thinking, more action, more final product, and of even greater importance more enhancement of human values. The leaders we need are men who can think clearly, who can accept facts without prejudice, who are open to new ideas, who can see problems and move in on them, who are cordial and warm in their personal relations, who know how to rally intelligent support for the good that is to be done, who can hate evil without hating the evildoer, who delight not in gaining power for themselves but in seeing more and more people become able and willing to carry responsibility."[9]

People can learn how to carry responsibility, as is illustrated by the following experience:

"The president and I met by appointment to discuss how to set up the Committee on Structure. Decided we would need to have in the group the executive committee of the board, plus the branch chairman, plus some others including staff. Some members of the executive committee are named in the bylaws, but the appointive ones have not been named. Decided we need to add program planning chairman, finance chairman, public relations and personnel. The membership chairman is one of the vice presidents at present. Miss F, who is second vice president and present chairman, seems the outstanding person to serve as chairman of the new committee. Why do we need the executive committee as core of the Structure Committee? Because they are a group most aware of the problems involved in our structure. They are long-time members of the agency and have been involved in many facets of it. They are the total picture. They meet the problems of others in trying to get work done. They ask the questions about channels and lines of communication. Why do we need the branch chairman on it? Because one big problem is that people in branches will accept responsibility in their branch but always resist and question it. They do not understand why

111

they have to participate in the whole. Also, the branches seem to lack knowledge about the necessity for central administration. We need the program planning, finance, personnel, and public relations represented because all of them meet the problems of the structure and are involved in the structure."

Ross and Hendry in their study of leadership summarize their findings by saying "the profile of the leader indicated by the research reported is that of a self-confident, well-integrated, emotionally stable individual; one who has a desire to lead and is willing, able, and competent in a particular situation; who is identified with the norms, values, and goals of the group of which he is the leader; who is a warm, sensitive, and sympathetic person, and able to help members in a practical way; who is intelligent relative to other group members; and who is consistent in performing his leadership functions. . . . Different situations will undoubtedly demand more or less of these qualities, but in general terms this profile represents as accurately as can be described at the present time that which the 'good' leader in our society must be."[10]

Self-Awareness and Self-Discipline

Administrative leaders must have a high degree of self-awareness and a greater than average amount of self-discipline. In discussing self-awareness Ronken and Lawrence define it as "an understanding of one's own frame of reference, together with active attention to the relationship process, which enables one also to take account of the other person's point of view. . . . Self-awareness . . . comes in part from knowing oneself well enough to discriminate in one's own behavior, for instance, the giving of a just criticism from 'taking it out on' the nearest subordinate. It comes from courage to recognize the emotional components of one's own attitudes and behavior, wisdom to realize that they may be a source of strength as well as of weakness, toleration for the differences between one's own point of view and someone else's, and faith that man has inside him the seeds of growth."[11]

In reviewing the disciplines essential in developing administrative skill Towle lists such items as (1) discrimination in terms of time and effort, (2) the use of agency routine to facilitate service efforts, (3) increasingly drawing on agency and community resources to get work done, (4) increasing capacity for professional relationships and to use the thinking of others, (5) ability to look beyond the immediate job and see the whole, (6) an understanding of one's own relationship to the agency, (7) flexibility which emerges from deep professional security.[12]

In discussing the psychological factors in administrative leadership Hanford lists a number of personal reactions that are likely to be felt by any person who is doing an administrative job. She suggests that the making of decisions which are likely to bring either blame or credit may arouse a certain amount of anxiety in the administrative leader. She says further that since the administrative leader must necessarily make evaluations of performance there may be hostility reactions from those being evaluated and these reactions may arouse fears in the administrator. She

113

urges the necessity of learning how to control personal responses and how to anticipate the responses of others. She stresses the fact that administrative leaders must have new ideas and express them, but do so in such a fashion that they do not seem to be imposed. She highlights the necessity for the administrative leader to set a good example in managing his own job and suggests that the staff will learn from this example. If people are held to a high standard the administrator himself must hold to high standards. She stresses the importance of steady supportive leadership, saying that "morale permeates from the executive down through, and good morale is based on an even confidence that the person at the top knows where he is going." She says, too, that administrative leaders must accept the two-way feelings that other people have toward folks in the leadership role; she suggests that while every administrative leader faces discouragements and fatigue it is better not to share these low moments with the staff; she stresses the idea that true leadership is not managing but is sensitivity.[13]

Authority in Administration

Walton states, "Not only is authority necessary for the administration of education; it is also legitimate. Its sources, which are legal, social, and personal, provide the positive power and the sanctions that make it effective . . . . By authority we mean simply the power and the recognized right of the administrator, enforced by whatever sanctions he may employ, to make decisions necessary for the co-ordination of the activities of persons working within an organization . . . Persons working in an organization accept the authority of the administrator because it is legal, because it is an accepted part of the culture, and because of certain traits in the administrator himself."[14]

It should be pointed out that authority is inherent in every job, that it goes with the function, the task, and the position. Furthermore the specific amount or degree of authority varies with the specific scope of the jobs involved. In addition, authority implies that the person has knowledge, experience, and background which qualify him to exercise it. Also it must be observed that in every organization authority is distributed and shared by many people. It implies trust, security, responsibility, and accountability. Authority is used to define and set limits on individual and group responsibility; furthermore it is useful in establishing methods, procedures, and policies for carrying out the work of the agency. Well-specified authority fosters coordination and agency wholeness.

It must be noted that administrative leaders have certain feelings about authority and oftentimes have difficulty in accepting the fact that they must use the authority vested in them and in their positions. Staff members and volunteers may likewise have difficulty understanding the important place of authority in every organization. In certain kinds of situations these feelings may become activated and intense enough to create "authority problems." Problems may arise from misunderstandings and from the failure on the part of administrative leaders to spell out precisely the degree of authority involved in the various positions.

Communication of Feelings and Values

The administrator carries a heavy responsibility for the communication of feelings and values between groups and individuals to help them find a common ground. In addition, the administrator is responsible for the communication of ideas, orally and in writing, to individuals, committees, groups, and organizations. Furthermore, he must be skillful in finding and preparing facts in usable form and must know how to help individuals and work groups do their own fact finding and properly use relevant facts. A vitally important responsibility of the administrator is that of helping individuals and work groups make responsible decisions. This means helping them with problem identification, sorting out of problems, seeing interrelationships among them, problem solving, and evaluating the consequences of proposed solutions. These are all related to the process of responsible decision making. Also administrative leaders must have an understanding of policy and program analysis coupled with skill in policy and standard formulation. These twin functions of analysis and formulation are fundamental to the administrator's ability to help a group analyze a problem and then make its own decision.

Lawrence points out, "The administrator has to live in a multidimensional world with a responsibility for taking action in leading people and in dealing with concrete problems. He must constantly seek multifunctional solutions. This forces him into many paradoxical situations. The administrator must constantly strive to maintain a consistency in his behavior while accepting the fact that his behavior will always appear inconsistent from any simple, one-dimensional frame of reference. He must constantly seek for solutions that resolve conflicts between the interests of several dimensions, but accept the fact that such conflicts are inevitable and never ending. He must constantly seek to change behavior in the social system. He must seek a perfection of balanced development but accept the inevitability of imperfection. He must place heavy emphasis upon achieving organization purposes and must maintain the perspective of an outside observer, but not lose his impassioned involvement with the results of the system."[15]

Toward a Deeper Understanding of Skill

Skillful administrative leaders have a considerable amount of self-understanding and self-awareness. They know their own frame of reference and give active attention to themselves in the relationship process; as they become secure in their leadership responsibilities they are able to exert more conscious effort in new situations. The conscious use of oneself represents a person's ability to control the emotional components of his own behavior and to deal sensitively with the feelings and attitudes of others. It takes skill to release and channel feelings and attitudes so that they become task focused and directed toward goals.

How the administrative leader behaves or works with the task group clearly affects its behavior and responses. The perception, understanding, and sensitivity toward the behavior of others which the administrative leader develops are an essential aspect of self-awareness. What the administrative leader sees in the situation, his judgments and inferences about it, tend to control his behavior. Skillful administrative leaders carry on a continuous assessment of the total situation. They endeavor to see the parts and the whole; in helping task groups see their specific responsibilities they continuously call attention to the way these fit into the total picture. Leaders who work skillfully help people become engaged or involved in a contributing way. Out of such contributions come movement, and the leader's role changes as the task group proceeds; this means that subsequent directions are determined not in a prearranged sequence but in relation to where the work group is and what it needs from leadership at the moment. Inasmuch as there are always many groups at work simultaneously the ramifications of their separate acts cannot be isolated but always have to be seen in relation to their effect upon the total situation. Thus the ongoing assessment calls for a frequent evaluative look at the specific task and at the total situation. Skilled administration calls for a well-developed sense of timing. Skill involves knowing when to wait and when to press ahead, when people may be receptive to ideas and when they may be reluctant to look at anything new, letting people move along at their own pace but at the same time stimulating them to move forward as they are able.

It takes time to build a network of relationships within which people can learn to communicate with one another and work together successfully in the solution of problems. Administrative leaders should be realistic about the amount of time required by people to carry through on complicated tasks.

The creative use of conflict is another aspect of skill. There are bound to be disagreements and conflicts between board and staff, staff and the community, members and the staff, and so on. Skillful administrators bring disagreements into the open and face the need to deal with them objectively, converting them into a creative experience for the participants whenever possible.

Skilled administrators have the ability to keep movement going on several fronts simultaneously. This calls for them to keep many individuals and groups interested over a long period of time while a goal is being worked for. Such skill involves holding the groups accountable for their assigned tasks and the ability to stimulate, direct, correlate, and evaluate the work as it proceeds. Interest, movement, and motivation are better sustained when certain things happen in advance preparation, scene setting, and in weeding out the important from the unimportant. Skill is manifested when administrative leaders work with people to help them become clearer in their thinking and more precise in their expression. The leader must frequently present material to boards and committees in such a way that it is understandable and so drafted that the board can take knowledgeable action.

Skillful administrative leaders take responsibility to provide a structure and to help people work within it. The structure should be the kind that makes involvement possible, but it should be no more extensive than necessary to carry on the work of the agency. A good structure is economical to manage from a time, money, and leadership standpoint. When structure is well constituted there will be an orderly flow of work, uniformity of procedure, and clearly defined areas of responsibility. Good structure provides for an orderly grouping of the various task forces with a reasonable rapid transmittal of information up and down as well as across the agency. Fundamentally, a good structure helps to improve morale and work satisfaction.

"Administrative leaders must have a considerable knowledge of the processes of change and how to help people understand the need for change and become receptive to it. This seems to be especially important when leaders deal with representatives of a portion of the agency and yet are charged with a responsibility of making decisions for the total agency. Every individual labors under the disadvantage of working with material that affects the whole even though he can see only a part of the agency. Hence, the administrative leader has to bring in a sense of wholeness and must emphasize the importance of planned, thoughtful, dynamic change for a better program of service."[16] A major and continuing area of responsibility for administrative leaders is in establishing and improving communication. The next chapter is devoted to this subject.

NOTES

1. Donald T. Campbell, *Leadership and Its Effect Upon the Group* (Columbus, Ohio: Ohio State University, 1956), p. 1.

2. Chester I. Barnard, *Organization and Management* (Cambridge, Mass.: Harvard University Press, 1948), p. 83.

3. Elton Mayo, *The Social Problems of an Industrial Civilization* (Boston, Mass.: Division of Research, Graduate School of Business Administration, Harvard University, 1945), p. 13.

4. *Leadership at Work* (Washington, D.C.: National Education Association, 1942), p. 21.

5. Robert N. McMurry, "Man-Hunt for Top Executives," *Harvard Business Review*, January–February, 1954.

6. Ordway Tead, "Reflections on the Art of Administration," *Hospital Administration,* Winter, 1959, p. 10.

7. John D. Glover and Ralph M. Hower, *The Administrator* (Homewood, Ill.: R. D. Irwin, 1952), pp. 2–3.

8. Margaret Logan Clark and Briseis Teall, *The Executive Director on the Job* (New York, N.Y.: The Woman's Press, 1947), p. 8

9. L. K. Hall, "What's New About Leaders and Leadership?" National Council of the YMCAs of the United States, 1953.

10. Murray G. Ross and Charles E. Hendry, *New Understandings of Leadership* (New York, N.Y.: Association Press, 1957), pp. 59–60.

11. Harriet O. Ronken and Paul R. Lawrence, *Administering Changes—A Case Study of Human Relations in a Factory* (Boston, Mass.: Harvard University, Division of Research, Graduate School of Business Administration, 1952), p. 310.

12. Charlotte Towle, "Professional Skill in Administration" *The News-Letter,* American Association of Psychiatric Social Workers, May, 1940, p. 11.

13. Jeannette Hanford, "Psychological Factors in Executive-Staff Relationships" in *Some Dynamics of Social Agency Administration* (New York, N.Y.: Family Service Association, 1946), pp. 55 ff.

14. John Walton, *Administration and Policy Making in Education"* (Baltimore, Md.: Johns Hopkins Press, 1959), pp. 106, 104.

15. Paul R. Lawrence, *The Changing of Organizational Behavior Patterns—A Case Study of Decentralization* (Cambridge, Mass.: Harvard University, Graduate School of Business, 1958), pp. 225–226.

16. Based on Harleigh B. Trecker, "Understandings of Administration," *The YWCA Magazine,* June, 1960, pp. 29–30.

CHAPTER **6**

Establishing and Improving Communication

COMMUNICATION has long been recognized as one of the essentials of good administration. Yet, far too often communication is faulty.

If one listens to the comments made by staff members and volunteers when communication is faulty here are some of the things that will be heard. "No one told me." "I wasn't consulted." "Why doesn't someone tell me these things?" "That's not the way I heard it." "Everyone interprets this bulletin differently." "Why don't people listen?" "Here we go again, too little and too late." All of these expressions indicate that the communication processes are not working effectively. In addition, it is easy to recall situations where poor writing or poor speaking resulted in misunderstanding and confusion. The same is true when administrators choose the wrong medium for communication and when their timing is bad. Oftentimes failure to assess the readiness of an individual or group to receive and respond to a communication is at fault. In other situations distortions of information occur as the information is passed through various channels. Meanings are altered and the responses are altered accordingly.

Sometimes administrators fail to assess the impact of communication in advance. They should ask themselves the question, what will this communication mean to the receiver? This is true with both written and oral items. In other circumstances people are swamped with too much material and they are not able to assimilate it quickly.

Communication problems may represent poor interpersonal relations, a lack of common language and values, or both. Also the failure on the part of people to distinguish between factual material and the interpretation of facts causes problems. In times of work pressure and in times of crisis communication problems are likely to be frequent. In many situations administrative leaders fail to test their communication material in advance, and as a result of this lack of a pre-test the item fails to accomplish its goal. In some situations the vague and nebulous material which is passed on fails to connect in the minds of the recipients and as a result nothing happens; it is not used.

In the light of the above it is apparent that *communication* is the very heart of co-operative undertakings. Many scholars of administration have stressed this.

Almost a quarter of a century ago Barnard observed, "The *first* executive function is to develop and maintain a system of communication."[1]

Bavelas and Barrett emphasize the importance of communication when they remark, "In an enterprise whose success hinges upon the co-ordination of the efforts of all its members, the managers depend completely upon the quality, the amount, and the rate at which relevant information reaches them. The rest of the organization, in turn, depends upon the efficiency with which the managers can deal with the information and reach conclusions, decisions, and so forth. . . . Communication is not a secondary or derived aspect of organization, a 'helper' of the other and more basic functions; rather it is the essence of organized activity and is the basic process out of which all other functions derive. The goals an organization selects, the methods it applies, the effectiveness with which it improves its own procedures—all of these hinge upon the quality and availability of the information in the system."[2]

Simon highlights the relationship between communication and decision making when he states, "Not only is communication absolutely essential to organization, but the availability of particular techniques of communication will in large part determine the way in which decision-making functions can and should be distributed throughout the organization. The possibility of permitting a particular individual to make a particular decision will often hinge on whether there can be transmitted to him the information he will need to make a wise decision, and whether he, in turn, will be able to transmit this decision to the other members of the organization whose behavior it is supposed to influence."[3]

Since communication is the major process of administration and since it is fundamental to all of the related and sub-processes, administrators must concentrate heavily on: understanding what communication means; learning how to establish a system of communication; and seeking not only to maintain but also to improve the system.

Understanding the Meaning of Communication

A first task is to think deeply into the meaning of communication and to define it operationally. Much help is available from recent formulations published in the literature of administration. Appley illuminates the concept when he says, "Communication is that process whereby one person makes his ideas and feelings known to another. It is the primary means whereby one influences others. . . . The manager who understands that his job is to make things happen realizes that he can make them happen only as he is able to establish sound objectives and methods in communication with others and, through effective communication, lead them to play the important role they must play. . . . Communication is a valuable skill and it runs through all of management."[4]

Communication between the president and the executive is especially important as is illustrated below:

"Communication between president and executive must be continuous and based on complete confidence in each other's intent; it must make use of telephone, memos, informal conversations, and planned conferences. Regular meetings in the office, if possible, are imperative because both organize their thoughts and questions for such discussions, and the documents they may need are at hand.

"When differences of opinion arise they should be talked out frankly and not allowed to simmer too long. If agreement on policy or important matters cannot be reached, the difference should be stated frankly in appropriate meetings so agency leaders can consider all points of view in making decisions. Such differences should be expected and not be allowed to affect the relationship of president and executive. Frankly faced, they give confidence to other leaders."

With reference to the field of educational administration but equally pertinent to the community service agency is Fisk's description of communication as "the ebb and flow of feelings and ideas among people. It is the reading, listening, speaking, writing, depicting; it is comprehending and making comprehensible that which one wishes to communicate. It is the desire to make one's feelings and ideas crystal clear to others. This is a highly important area of administrative behavior which should be developed."[5] Gregg elaborates on this theme when he observes, "Communication is the process by which directions, information, ideas, explanations, and questions are transmitted from person to person or from group to group. It is a process of interaction between or among individuals. The essential elements of an organization are common purpose, individuals willing to contribute to this purpose, and communication. Without communication there can be no purpose commonly understood and accepted nor can there be co-ordinated efforts of those contributing to that purpose."[6]

In their summary of new understandings of leadership Ross and Hendry put forth the thesis that to facilitate communication administrative leaders must concentrate more and more upon the group and the group's methods of work because "the essence of communication is the development of mutual understanding in the group, so that objectives and goals as they are developed have relevance and meaning for each member of the group. . . . Where there is effective communication there seems to be a greater mutual understanding, more friendliness, greater cohesion and greater potentiality for productivity."[7]

Communication between the executive and staff is pointed out in the illustration which follows:

"I presented the plan for the agency study to the administrative staff and interpreted its purpose and how it would work. I explained why we had appointed a consultant to the study committee and asked for opinions and comments. I did these things because it was important for the administrative staff to be aware of this committee's function, as they would be asked to participate. The success of the study depended upon the co-operative participation of the staff. I wanted them to be interested and at the beginning to see where they were essential. I told them that I would need their opinions from time to time and that I would report the committee's work to them."

The Communication System

From the foregoing descriptive definitions it would appear that a system of communication must be deliberately planned and requires considerable direction from administrative leadership to get it established. Furthermore communication seems to be made up of a number of elements which must be understood. These elements include:

1. Who are the communicators? Or who must be in continuous communication in our agency?

2. What is the content of communication or what is it that must be communicated?

3. Why is this content being communicated or what is the goal or reason for communicating this material? What decisions will it enable us to reach?

4. When must this content be communicated in terms of total timing of agency operations?

5. How should this content be communicated? Or what means or methods of communicating do we have at our disposal?

6. Where are the channels or networks both formal and informal in our organization which should be used to facilitate communication? The ways and means of communication must be based upon a clear understanding of the purposes sought, the nature of the material to be communicated or solicited, and of course the persons involved.

There are two broad categories to be considered: the first is that of spoken material and the second is that of written material. The spoken word is obvious in face-to-face contact such as interviews, conferences, committee meetings, staff meetings, board meetings, and the like. The same is true with telephone conversations, oral reports, and other verbal forms. Written communications are extensive in all agencies. Here, reference is made to letters, memoranda, bulletins, minutes of meetings, manuals, job specifications and descriptions, annual reports, survey reports, news releases, house publications, bulletin board items and so on.

It is interesting to study the modern agency and endeavor to list what it is that is being communicated. Certainly high on the list would be material related to the goals of the agency, its methods of work, and its philosophy of giving services. In addition, policy material, procedural material, and program material are constantly communicated throughout the agency. Assignments, responsibilities, and the conditions and limitations attached to assignments and responsibilities are likewise important.

In another instance the executive takes initiative to assure good communication and states her role clearly: "I asked the special consultant who was helping us with this project to talk with me about plans for the committee meeting. As executive director, it is my job to further communication between the chairman and staff of the center and members of the public relations committee and to assist in defining their roles in relation to the work that is to be done."

Agreements, plans, and general information are constantly flowing throughout the communication channels. In addition, it is important to point out that reports, statistics, all related to services are constantly being communicated. Workers particularly should be invited to offer their suggestions for change; they should report the problems that they are encountering and they should indicate the way policies and procedures are working out.

Program developments need to be considered, as do all inquiries for information and all plans for the future.

The material mentioned above is passing through the various channels of communication in the agency. The regular channels are those specified in the formal organization. In addition to the formal organization there are many informal social contacts which give opportunity for communication. Individual conferences, group meetings, and events in the community are important channels to utilize for particular purposes.

The form of organization is exceedingly important at this point. If it is basically a sound structure the formal channels of communication will be used and there will be less need to utilize the informal grapevine.

An executive describes how the agency structure is supposed to provide for communication but could be improved:

"The metropolitan structure provides that communication between branches and metropolitan is carried largely by attendance of branch representatives at metropolitan meetings and by attendance of president or alternates and executive at branch meetings and events. This latter places a burden on the president and executive and a plan should be made so both do not attend the same meetings. There needs to be far better communication between chairmen of metropolitan committees and their counterparts in the branches, since at the moment branch executives and the metropolitan executives are largely carrying branch-metropolitan relationships."

The basic characteristics of community service agencies must be taken into account in establishing the communication system. Very often these agencies bring together several professional disciplines and this means that there are specialized languages which must be understood and sufficiently shared so that common meanings may be attached to words and phrases. In addition, many community service agencies perform a number of functions. These multiple function agencies are inclined to have specialized departments responsible for rendering specialized services. Under these circumstances communication may be hazardous and may be particularly difficult to develop across specialized lines. Another aspect is the basic composition of professional and volunteer workers, who carry responsibility but may not always have a common and unified understanding of the agency.

Of great importance is the fact that the community service agency often renders intangible services. This makes for difficulty in creating clear understandings not only of purpose but of the methods used. Communication must rest upon shared ideas, concepts, and principles of professional practice. All too often these kinds of ideological materials are difficult for persons to understand and utilize. Furthermore, in the services of our community agencies much of what is done for the assistance of the individual is confidential and personal in nature. Under these circumstances some of the explanatory background material must necessarily remain the private property of the professional worker and cannot be shared with others. Another factor in the agency situation is the series of relationships it must maintain with a wide variety of other agencies. Here, the complications of internal communication are multiplied when decisions have to be made in concert with other agencies which likewise have particular internal communication aspects.

The larger the agency the more complicated is the communication problem. This is particularly true in the decentralized agency where there may be a considerable distance between the central authority and the operating units which are far out on the periphery.

Budget and financial data must be communicated if programs are to be well planned. In a thoughtful description of program review in relation to costs we find these insights:

"The executive director suggested that the program planning committee have an all-day meeting with the three branches and the center to review their programs. The metropolitan program director developed a schedule of activities; the comptroller worked with her to show program content in relation to cost. This was the first such analysis this committee had seen, and as the members put the information on a large board they gained new insight into the total program. Gaps, lack of balance, and quality were shown as they recommended continuation or elimination of units.

"It was a revealing session, and the interaction of staff and volunteers was exciting. Vested interests, professional status, antagonisms, lack of appreciation of the total agency, concern for budget and its relation to the quality of program, community changes and their effect on the program focus were elements of this review."

The agency itself, if it is a part of a central organization or if it is a part of a regional or a national organization has additional communication channels to establish and maintain. Likewise it should be pointed out that most agencies today are affiliated with central planning units and this makes for an increase in the need to communicate with others. If the agency has a rigorous hierarchical form of organization this too makes for difficulty in communication.

Still another factor to be considered is the changing personnel situation in many agencies; when there is a rapid turnover of staff or volunteers, communication must be learned by newcomers and must be reviewed by those who continue with the agency. The more familiarity a person has with the agency the easier it will be for him to communicate with his colleagues and with his clients. Not only does personnel change; programs and services change too. This means that special attention has to be given to communication efforts designed to acquaint people with the changes in agency services. When changes are regarded as favorable by the persons served, communication will be considerably quicker and easier. Under those circumstances where changes may seem to result in a probable loss of service or of status then a different approach will have to be used. It is generally regarded that when a group to whom one is communicating is friendly the communication process is vastly more comfortable and easy than when unfriendly recipients are awaiting the word.

None of the above is to suggest that the community service agency is any more or less difficult from the standpoint of communication than any other agency. It is, however, different and it should be understood in the light of its special factors and considerations.

Improving Communication

When administrators take a critical look at the who, what, why, when, how, and where of communication in their agencies they often realize that communication may be effective and productive or the opposite may be the case. If they are to improve the system they must first locate the problems in it.

Among the frequently stated problems of communication are: *First,* quite often the wrong people are in communication with one another. *Second,* there is a failure to screen out and select important and relevant material to be communicated. *Third,* there is often a lack of clarity as to the goal or reason for communicating particular materials. *Fourth,* there is a lack of clarity of expression and misunderstanding of the meaning of terms. *Fifth,* there may be a faulty structure or the failure to utilize existing channels which are spelled out in the structure. *Sixth,* timing is faulty, and the length of time it takes to carry through a communication is increasingly burdensome.

As has been emphasized, a central responsibility of administrators is the establishment, development, and improvement of communication throughout the entire agency, or throughout the section, division, or department which is the special province of the person in charge.

Assuming that administrators have the responsibility not only to establish and maintain but also to improve communication in their organizations, what are some of the things that can be done?

First, they will assess periodically with individuals and

groups on their staff, boards, committees, and constituencies how they feel about the communication system and process and what suggestions they would offer for improving it.

Second, they will evaluate the content of communication, particularly written material, to ascertain its impact and the extent to which its accomplishes its purposes.

Third, they will review the channels of communication to be sure that they are really open at all times and are being utilized efficiently.

Fourth, in so far as possible basic major terms and words used will be defined and spelled out so that people will attach comparable meaning to them.

Fifth, in obvious cases of communication breakdown—and they do happen everywhere—a careful evaluation will be made to see what were some of the reasons for the failure. When there is a failure in communication the administrative leader must try to discover why and endeavor to remedy the situation:

"In a meeting of the board and staff the chairman of the public relations committee reported on activities and was not very clear in her presentation. Furthermore, the staff members could not be of assistance because of lack of understanding of the relationship of the staff to the public relations committee. This points up that communication has failed. Staff members do not understand their role. The chairman has not been regular in attendance at meettings, and she failed to clear with the staff members before making the report."

In another situation a president deliberately made an opportunity for a board member to communicate her feelings, which had been only partly revealed in a board meeting:

"I called Mrs. T to learn, if possible, the source of ire she expressed at the board meeting. She was distressed over the lack of program in our Northeast Center and the lack of use of the building. I wanted to let her talk herself out, hoping that then she would turn her energy to constructive use in developing a plan to serve this section with its new population. She is a valuable person with deep conviction."

Sixth, they will be more conscious of the difference in frames of reference that people have and will strive to educate for agreement on basic frames of reference.

Seventh, they will document, manualize, and proceduralize agreements so that persons will have reference material.

Eighth, they will try to shorten the lines of communication and be more conscious of the importance of timing.

Ninth, they will reduce the number of bottlenecks or blocking points in the communication channels and seek for a free flow of information. After doing the things mentioned above, skillful administrators will make an over-all evaluation of the communication system in terms of criteria of effectiveness.

Some of the characteristics of effective communication can be listed as follows:

First, the purpose of the communication must be clear and must be understood by the person making the communication and by the person receiving it.

Second, both spoken and written material must be as

clear as possible and subject to one and only one interpretation. If it is not possible to be this precise, every effort should be made to reduce the number of exceptions or options that are left open at the point of interpretation.

Third, effective communication is a series of consistent acts. In other words, subsequent communications are consistently related to earlier communications and avoid the hazard of being in conflict or canceling out.

Fourth, good communication is adequate to accomplish its purpose; it is neither too much nor too little; it has a sharp focus and is selective as to content.

Fifth, good communication is timely in that thought is given to the timing at point of issue and the readiness on the part of the recipient.

Sixth, in good communication thought is given to the channels to be utilized and to the distribution, so that the right persons will receive the material. This usually requires a system which will make for not only downward and upward communication but lateral communication as well.

In discussing the real goal of communication Tead suggests that it is "successful operationally only when it is seen in its true moral depth. . . . The effort of communication is the effort at bottom to change in some degree the life of somebody else. That is what it comes down to basically. You are changing, you want to change, some idea, some attitude, some process, some way of attacking problems, in respect to a group or an individual to whom the communication is being addressed. Communication is productive only on the assumption that there is a sharing of ideas, of attitudes, of policies, of whatever it is for which the change is sought. Unless there is a change in the attitude, a change in the conduct, there is no communication. . . . You can have all the house organs, all of the bulletins, all the other convenient and useful gadgets of communication, and have no communication. There has to be on the part of the communicator, the most prayerful consideration of the means by which and the appraisal and estimate by which one knows that desire has been sparked and a favorable response will be forthcoming. . . . Communication is always the touching of mind to mind, of person to person, whether it is one man to a thousand diverse individuals, or one man to thirty in a single department. This process can be many things, including conversation, interview, dialogue, visual impress, all if they yield an interaction of one personality upon another. Hopefully the interaction will be affirmative and new agreements will be achieved. Active consent is the important end."[8]

In the next chapter we will consider the processes of planning and co-ordination. These processes are rooted in the over-all communication system of the agency.

NOTES

1. Chester I. Barnard, *The Functions of the Executive* (Cambridge, Mass.: Harvard University Press, 1938), p. 226.

2. Alex Bavelas and Dermott Barrett, "An Experimental Approach to Organizational Communication," *Personnel*, XXVII (1951) 368.

3. Herbert A. Simon, *Administrative Behavior: A Study of the Decision-Making Processes in Administrative Organizations* (New York, N.Y.: The Macmillan Co., 1957), p. 154.

4. Lawrence A. Appley, *Management in Action* (New York, N.Y.: American Management Association, 1956), pp. 182–183.

5. Robert S. Fisk, "The Task of Educational Administration" in Roald F. Campbell and Russell T. Gregg, *Administrative Behavior in Education* (New York, N.Y.: Harper & Brothers, 1957), p. 204.

6. Russell T. Gregg, "The Administrative Process" in Campbell and Gregg, *op. cit.*, p. 294.

7. Murray Ross and Charles E. Hendry, *New Understandings of Leadership* (New York, N.Y.: Association Press, 1957), p. 79.

8. Ordway Tead, "Reflections on the Art of Administration," *Hospital Administration*, Winter, 1959, pp. 13–14.

CHAPTER 7

Planning and Co-ordination

In the previous chapter on communication it was pointed out that administrative leaders have a continuing responsibility for giving leadership to the major processes used by the agency in accomplishing its purposes. In this chapter we will discuss the nature and importance of: planning, or what is involved in laying out the work of the agency; and co-ordination, or relating the work of various individuals and groups.

Planning helps the agency know where it is going and why. Planning helps the agency know whether it is in step with community needs and community attitudes. Administrative planning consists of determining the needs that require planned action, spelling out the opportunities for service and the requirements if service is to be given. In addition, administrative planning calls for the evaluating of alternate courses of action. A good plan indicates what is to be accomplished, how it is to be accomplished, who is responsible, what are the resource requirements, and what are the methods of evaluation and review.

Definitions of Planning

Walters' definition of planning is broad and inclusive. He says, "planning is pre-thinking, thinking up, thinking out, and thinking through. . . . It includes pre-thinking what and how to do it—the thinking through of the course and methods of action. It is the thinking part of administration before action—the going through of the action in the mind. It is the looking ahead, the foresight, the forecasting, to assess the future probabilities and decide what to do and what is to be done in view of the possibilities. It is the conceiving, defining, and preparation of the purposes, policies, the procedures, duties to be performed in advance of their organization, management, appraisal, and control. Planning is laying out and charting the administrative process. It involves research. The facts must be obtained before the plan and plans can be made. It is systematic and orderly arrangement of the steps of the administrative process; the actions and sub-actions, the process and sub-processes to be carried out from the beginning to the end."[1]

In very clear terms Beavers defines planning as "working out in broad outlines the things that need to be done and the methods for doing them." With like simplicity she defines co-ordinating as "the interrelating of the various parts of the work."[2]

An over-all plan gives focus and direction to group effort and provides for co-ordination, as is illustrated by this excerpt from a record kept by an executive:

"The executive director, assistant executive, and president met to work on committee chairmanships for next year. We proposed only one assignment but had a thorough review of the entire situation. We discussed the size of the committees, wondering whether in many cases a team of an able volunteer and related staff member might not be more effective than a committee. We decided that the role of the program planning committee should be redefined and each new problem it undertakes carefully examined in light of its proposed function. Otherwise it will continue as it has been, taking on any job that falls into its path just because no other committee or staff group is handling it."

Characteristics of Good Planning

One of the leading management consultants emphasizes the fact that planning is "that phase of management that establishes the future course of an enterprise. . . . Actually planning is management itself projected into the future. It has been defined as an attempt by an agency to establish rational control over its own destiny. . . . An agency is engaged in planning when it (1) selects and defines its objectives—in other words, defines its role, (2) determines the programs required to fulfill its role, and (3) develops time-phased plans for systematic achievement of those objectives.

"A review of planning practices in some of the more successfully managed agencies reveals a number of characteristics that seem to be prevalent in all good planning. *One,* it appears that planning is a top management function that cannot be delegated or neglected without serious detrimental effects on the agency. If top management gives up the planning function, it in fact gives up leadership of the agency. *Two,* planning begins today and extends into the future. It cannot be involved with the distant future only, for today's decisions shape tomorrow's agency. *Three,* planning should be orderly. It moves in a reasonable fashion from objectives to the programs required for the attainment of goals—it moves logically from objectives to integrated programs for implementation. It cannot be wholly casual or informal. *Four,* effective planning should result in definite goals, programs, responsibilities, and relationships. Its results should be quite tangible. The increasing demands for agency services, the changing nature of the services required, and rapidly increasing cost pressures all accent the need for down-to-earth, practical planning.

"*Five,* planning is also dynamic. It takes into account changing conditions and new developments and makes corresponding adjustments to accommodate changes. It must be firm enough to provide guidance, but flexible enough to meet the agency's changing needs. Planning should be not an administrative strait jacket, but a flexible tool for helping an agency to define and achieve its objectives. *Six,* planning should be action oriented. It is not an end in itself, not just a blueprint, but a means to an end. It leads to effective action and positive accomplishment. It follows that planning must be done in a way that the process of determining objectives and programs actually helps to generate the action required for achievement. In order to be fully effective, it must carry within itself the seeds of accomplishment. It is thus apparent that planning is not an exercise in abstract speculation or wishful thinking, but a living experience in purposeful teamwork. It is a planned activity in which the activity itself affects the plans."[3]

In assessing the characteristics of a good plan persons should ask the following questions as outlined by Seckler-Hudson: "Is the plan based on clearly defined dimensions and objectives? Is the plan as clear and simple as the subject matter will permit? Does the plan have stability while providing for flexibility? Does the plan outline standards of operation or clearly provide for them? Is the plan economical in terms of resources needed to implement it? Is the plan needed? Does the plan anticipate the future?"[4]

One executive reports: "The president and the executive director agreed to request authorization from the board of directors to create a special committee on staff-development. We set up criteria and qualifications for membership on this committee to get the right people for the job to be done. We took these steps because we thought they were good administrative procedures and also to insure that the board would feel responsible for the project."

With candor one volunteer admits that poor planning was a factor in a meeting which did not develop as she had hoped: "The program planning committee met for a confused two and a half hours. Lack of clear thinking on its function and lack of planning came to the surface, along with the feeling on the part of the branch that the committee has no power of decision on priorities. Therefore, it isn't important for the branch to be represented by more than its executive, who is supposed to come anyway. Much ambivalence and some discomfort, but it is well to get these feelings out."

The essence of planning and co-ordination comes out in this excerpt from a president's record: "Taking the initiative to keep a piece of work moving through the planning process is one of the primary responsibilities of the president and executive director. New ideas come from many sources, which must be tested and adapted or discarded by whatever group or groups are responsible. Once a plan is accepted, the president and executive need to consider the timing, the delegation of responsibility, and how to bring to bear the resources of the agency and the community toward its accomplishment. They must estimate what problems are important and pressing and how many projects can be undertaken at once."

The results of good planning show up in the way the task groups come to grips with their problems: "A great deal of thought and time were given to planning. We felt we had been making good progress, and the group members seemed to have reached a meeting of minds. Not that they were all agreed about what to do, but they had defined some of the problems. They now seemed able to say, 'These are the things that bother us. Let's see how we can approach them and what we can do about them. These are the areas where we agree. These are the things on which we don't agree and should study further.' "

What lies back of a good plan or good planning? What has the administrator done to make it a good plan? It is

145

likely that the administrator has made a clear analysis of the past experience of the agency and has taken a detailed look at the present situation including trends in service. In addition the planful administrator has been thinking ahead and has been making regular forecasts based on facts when they are available, or on estimates when the factual picture is incomplete. This administrator is anticipating the future needs of the agency rather than merely awaiting the future. In addition the planful administrator has assembled all relevant material and has made material available in a form that is understandable to all concerned who must participate in decision making. In addition, the planful administrator has a good sense of time and timing and knows how to schedule activity so that plans are realistic in relation to resources.

Co-ordination

Co-ordination is a very important part of the job of the administrator. As reported in a recent discussion, "It is his responsibility to help staff members see how their jobs fit into the total organization and how their functions in the organization affect the operation of related departments and the organization as a whole. . . . One of the administrator's major problems is to help each staff member to see his task as a component part of the total organization and as contributing to over-all organizational goals."[5]

Most agencies are organized, for operating purposes, into divisions and sub-divisions to distribute the work and to increase the efficiency of services. Ordinarily, like functions are grouped together into harmonious and systematic patterns. This grouping provides not only a structure within which the agency may operate but a framework within which the various operations are co-ordinated. Co-ordination thus is the activity that deals with interrelating the various parts of the work of the enterprise. It is only natural and human for individuals to place considerable stress on the importance of the area of work with which they are most closely identified. Their regular duties and regular responsibilities loom large to them. They may see them as having greater significance than is really the case. Thus, co-ordination can help workers to understand other divisions or other parts of the agency and help them to relate their work to these parts.

As Simon observes "The effectiveness of an individual in achieving his aims in any social situation will depend not only upon his own activity, but also on how well that activity relates to what the other individuals concerned are doing. . . . Viewed from the position of the individual in organization, co-ordination involves several elements: the relation of the individual's objectives and intermediate aims to those of other segments of the organization; the individual's assessment of the alternatives available to him and to the other members of the group; and his expectations as to the courses of action that will be followed by the others."[6]

An executive is carrying a co-ordination responsibility when she reports: "Met again with the administrative staff and brought them up to date on the progress of the pilot interviewers, saying they had an interesting evening of training and were now getting into their interviews. Asked them to give any assistance they could in suggesting whom they might interview. We discussed the variation of members and electors whom we wanted to participate. Again, this was a matter of co-ordination and bringing the administrative staff along with us on the project, soliciting their help and suggesting persons to interview, getting a variety as to age and experience in the members or electors in the pilot interviewing. The time schedule was made clear to them when the pilot project was to be completed."

Here an executive stresses the importance of follow-up as a part of co-ordination: "I called each person and asked whether all of her finance campaign cards had been distributed and what problems she was having in getting them out. This is one step in carrying the administration of the project and keeping the person responsible informed. It is a way of getting quickly at any problems, making adjustments to meet them, facilitating the process, and keeping it from bogging down."

It should be pointed out that the purpose of administrative co-ordination is to enable the total agency to carry on its operation in the most productive way possible so as to achieve its goals with maximum efficiency. Furthermore, the principal means of achieving administrative co-ordination is through the voluntary co-operative efforts of the individuals engaged in carrying out the organization's work. The administrator brings about voluntary co-operative efforts through the development of incentives to function co-operatively. Administrative co-ordination depends on the establishment of a purposeful relationship between the administrative leader and the members of the various work groups. Such a relationship is based on mutual understanding and acceptance of the administrative leader as the person carrying final responsibility for the operation of the total agency. In addition, there is mutual understanding and acceptance of the staff as responsible members of the administrative group who share with the executive the goal of building a co ordinated work force. Obviously, administrative co-ordination is dependent on understanding and on the exchange of information and knowledge. This means that there must be a system of communication that makes possible a back and forth transmission of knowledge and understanding throughout the entire agency. In addition, administrative co-ordination depends upon a high degree of compatibility among the individuals carrying on the various operations.[7]

The executive committee is another means of co-ordination: "The executive and president, working with the executive committee, have adopted a helpful procedure. When the program or any other committee votes to propose an important matter to the board, it is asked to take it to the executive committee first for consideration of how the plan may be supported by staff, facilities, and funds. One function of the executive committee is to fit the details of leadership, finance, and resources into program planning."

In the next chapter work with boards and committees will be discussed.

NOTES

1. J. E. Walters, *Basic Administration* (Paterson, N.J.: Littlefield, Adams & Co., 1959), pp. 4–5.

2. Helen D. Beavers, *Administration in the YWCA* (New York, N.Y.: The Woman's Press, 1944), p. 6.

3. Arnold F. Emch, "Planning for Health and Welfare Agencies." A paper presented at the 1959 Convention, The National Society for Crippled Children and Adults, November 30, 1959, Chicago, Illinois.

4. Catheryn Seckler-Hudson, "Planning—Basis for Future Action," *The Newsletter,* Girl Scouts of the U.S.A., New York, January, 1958.

5. *Professional Administrators for America's Schools,* 38th Yearbook, 1960 (Washington, D.C.: American Association of School Administration, National Education Association), pp. 121–122.

6. Herbert Simon, *Administrative Behavior: A Study of the Decision-Making Processes in Administrative Organizations* (New York, N.Y.: The Macmillan Co., 1957), pp. 103–104.

7. Based on Katherine Booth, *The Development of Administrative Co-ordination in the Executive Staff Meetings of a Social Agency.* Master of Social Work Thesis, University of Southern California, June, 1950. Unpublished.

CHAPTER **8**

Work with Boards, Committees, and Members

A SUBSTANTIAL PORTION of executive time is devoted to work with the board and committees. Some would suggest that this work is one of the most important things that the executive does. Most would agree that to be effective an agency must have an effective board. To have an effective board there must be good leadership from both the president and the executive. In this chapter attention will be directed toward administrative responsibility for boards, committees, and to some extent agency members or constituents. Inasmuch as boards of community service agencies are composed of volunteers, a brief review of the volunteer in community service is an appropriate starting place for the discussion. The extent to which the place of volunteers is clearly defined and understood is basic to administration.

The Volunteer in Community Service

When community service agencies are compared with business enterprises one of the distinct differences is in the realm of volunteer leadership and service. Most community service agencies, both voluntary and governmental and in various fields, are making an increasing use of volunteers. Volunteer services refer to the voluntary effort given without pay by any individual in a community who wishes to share in the responsibilities of those community institutions concerned with the advancement of community welfare. Voluntary services are a basic part of the American way of doing things. Volunteers are for the most part people with deep human service motivations. They are intelligent people who know how to do a job and if they do not know they are generally willing to accept training, for they are willing to learn. They are interested in their volunteer responsibilities, but, more important, they have conviction about the purpose, worth, and essential importance of what they are doing. Effective volunteers are people who can work with other people in a teamwork relationship.

Volunteers need clear-cut, defined jobs related to their abilities, experience, and competencies. They expect agency administration to provide proper training, instruction, orientation, and help in doing their jobs. They want the support and guidance of supervision and they expect evaluation. They want recognition and they need to be told that a good job has been done. Administrative leaders are responsible for seeing to it that volunteers understand the relationship of the job they do, however small, to the total agency effort. They must be made to feel the importance of their contribution. They must have opportunities to learn and to grow and they must work in a friendly, warm atmosphere where efforts are obviously needed and appreciated. Important as these things are, volunteers must have a real voice in determining goals and policies. As Cohen puts it, "Expansion of the role of the volunteer involves more than the question of numbers. A large number of people who are merely task involved without an understanding of the purpose and values of the program and without an opportunity to participate in the determining of goals and policies will not meet the need for maintaining our basic democratic fabric. The volunteer experience should provide, along with the feeling of being valued as an individual, a chance for meaningful participation and an intensification of a sense of social responsibility."[1]

A wise executive includes volunteers in the early planning of projects as did this one:

"Talked with the president and the chairman of the Home-Finding Committee, and proposed a meeting with the West Hamilton community people. Reported their interest and willingness to work together on this problem. I was interested in providing for the inclusion of appropriate agency volunteers in the *early thinking* about this project. It is very important to have the neighborhood people included because of their particular responsibility."

In some cases it is felt by volunteers that professional workers stand in the way of their assuming real responsibilities:

"All staff were invited to attend the meeting of the Committee on Services. This was a most revealing and interesting discussion. Everyone is aware of terrific changes around us and talks about the need for changes, and the staff members seem to be the most resistant to change! One volunteer suggested maybe staff stand in the way of volunteers' taking as much responsibility as they can. This provoked discussion of just what is the function of the staff and what is the function of the volunteer."

In the case of both professional workers and volunteer workers, it must be assumed that the tasks will be carried on with a high degree of competence. Further, to define the role of the professional worker, we must also define the role of the volunteer worker. The professional worker is prepared by education and experience to bring special skills to the job, and the employing body hires this professional worker to carry out work which has been defined and authorized by the policy-making body. Actually, the role must be determined in relation to the policy-making body, in relation to other staff members, and in relation to the clientele or constituency that his agency exists to serve. In addition to being responsible for carrying out the decisions authorized by the policy-making body, the professional worker also has the responsibility to bring to the policy-making board information needed by them to arrive at sound policy judgments. He must help the policy-making group to arrive at the best possible decisions.

In a recent study of volunteers the investigators Blumberg and Arsenian looked into many questions, one of which was why do people volunteer? They reported, "The primary reasons, in order of importance, given for their present involvement by both board members and group leaders were these: asked by another member or professional worker; a sense of civic duty; previous agency experience; and a liking for a particular activity. If one reads between the lines an assumption can be made that relatively few people simply walk into an organization, uninvited, and proceed to offer their services. The "asking" process must take place first. But who can be asked with some assurance that they will give an affirmative answer? On the face of it, it would seem that a person should be singled out who is known to have a sense of civic duty, has had previous experience in the agency, or who enjoys certain kinds of activities. This might be a step in the right direction, but it is only a step. That is, if a list of potential volunteers is narrowed down to those who fall into the above categories we may stand a better chance of securing their services, but the securing of a list of the most likely prospects, as has been pointed out, does not help too much unless they perceive that they will be able to achieve some needed satisfaction through the offering of their time and energy. People are not motivated in a vacuum. Nor do we "motivate" others. . . . If people come to see that they can get certain important needs satisfied by being a particular kind of volunteer they will, so to speak, motivate themselves. . . .

"The five most important satisfactions gained by Board members, in order of their importance, were a feeling of being of service, fellowship, a sense of upholding one's civic duty, being part of a developing institution, and having one's belief in the agency's purpose re-enforced."[2]

Boards as Administrative Volunteers

In Chapter 5 it was pointed out that administrative volunteers include agency presidents or board chairmen, officers, committee leaders, and board members. These boards are an essential and indispensable part of agency operations and administration. Their responsibilities and duties are broad and inclusive. It is generally agreed that boards have the following duties:

1. Establishing, clarifying, and modifying the purposes of the agency. It is the job of the board to state clearly what is the function of the agency, what its goals are, and what kinds of services it will offer; then the board must make certain that these services are being offered and that these goals are being attained. Of course, it becomes necessary from time to time for the board to modify the purposes and alter the services to meet changed conditions.

2. Planning the formal organization and structure is another board responsibility. It must see to it that the agency is properly organized to do its job and of course it must make sure that all state, local, and federal laws are observed.

3. The board has the major responsibility for seeing to it that the agency has the necessary facilities, staff, and material resources that are needed by it to conduct

its program. This is a never-ending job as programs expand and as additional resources are needed.

4. Policy making is, of course, a primary duty of the board. It must prescribe the conditions under which services will be provided as well as the basic policies for the entire operation of the agency. Policy making is likewise a never-ending task, because as conditions change policies must be revised, reformulated, and restated.

5. The board is always responsible for employing the executive and for determining his duties, compensation, and so on. After employment the board must delegate to the executive the necessary authority to administer the work of the agency. In addition, the board must evaluate the work of the executive.

6. Another responsibility of the board is to provide adequate finances so that the agency can carry on its program. This means working with the executive in setting the budget and in securing the money and guaranteeing the proper expenditure of all funds.

7. The board has the major responsibility in interpreting the services of the agency to the community. In this respect, board members are in a position to exercise considerable influence toward helping the community understand what the agency is trying to do.

8. Another responsibility of the board is to participate wholeheartedly in the community's efforts to plan for an adequate program of human services.

Board and Staff Must Work Together

It has been assumed earlier that the board and staff of the agency constitute the leadership team. In essence, it is agreed that board and staff members working together are responsible to the community for the satisfactory operation of the agency. It is further assumed that board members and staff members have specific responsibilities as well as common, shared responsibilities. Certainly, all board members and all staff members must be fundamentally motivated in and committed to the human services. As far as the staff is concerned, their primary role is that of carrying out or providing the program of services which the agency is set up to offer. For the board, their chief responsibility is that of providing the conditions under which the agency may render these services in terms of high quality. To some extent, there is an overlapping of responsibility between board and staff. In fact, in the modern community agency no longer is the board thought of as completely separated from the staff. Increasingly, there are tasks where board and staff members must work together. It is also assumed that communication is very important in the working together of board and staff. In fact, it is certain that board and staff members must be able to talk to one another about the major concerns of the agency if they are to see and accept their responsibilities. Furthermore, board members and staff members have much to learn from each other. There is a never-ending stream of new knowledge which must be shared.

The following are areas of shared responsibility which can be listed:

1. A major responsibility of board members and staff members is to understand and have conviction about the purpose and function of their agency. The word conviction is the key to the matter. Board members especially must feel deeply about the importance of what their agency is doing and must be willing to express this conviction steadfastly and firmly.

2. It is the responsibility of both groups to be thoroughly informed about the program and services of the agency and be willing to interpret these services widely so that more and more people will understand them.

3. Board members and staff members must work very hard to guarantee that the agency is provided with the conditions essential to the rendering of good service. Conditions include adequate budget, adequate staff, and adequate facilities, so that the agency will be allowed to offer a high quality of service always in relation to the best of standards.

4. It is important that the board members and staff members work together in appraising the work of the agency. In doing so they will make a conscious and continuous effort to be certain that the agency is doing the best possible job.

5. It is vital that board members and staff members have vision and imagination. Both groups should be looking ahead and trying to make plans for needs before the needs become so acute that the agency is overwhelmed by them. Long-range planning is par-

ticularly important today, and it is a shared responsibility.

6. Board members and staff members together have a responsibility to unite with the total community in formulating a philosophy of human needs and in suggesting how these needs should be met. There will always be honest differences of opinion as to how needs should be met. Nevertheless, board and staff members should be in the front line helping the community to make sound decisions.

7. It is the responsibility of all board members and staff members to study, to learn, to accept training so that they will be better equipped to do their jobs.

The Role of the Executive and the President

The persons who carry major responsibility for work with and leadership of the agency board are the *executive* and the *president*. Between them they must provide guidance, stimulation, direction, and continuing assistance so that the board will be able to carry out its tasks. Frequent mention is made of the fact that the *roles* of the executive and the president must be clearly defined and understood by both parties and by the board. However, it is not always clear as to what is meant by *role* as a term or concept. Before an attempt to prescribe the specific details of executive and presidential roles the concept itself should be examined.

The concept of role has its origins in the social sciences. A number of working definitions are available in the literature. In recent years, professional workers have begun to make use of role theory as one means of deepening their understandings of their professional responsibility in particular situations.

Several selected definitions of role as given by prominent authorities follow:

From the work of Maas: "Role may be defined as the institutionalized group expectations as to the behavior, attitudes, and other attributes for the occupant of a given position in a social system. . . . Expectations vary according to the position the individual occupies in a family, a work situation, or a school. For example, expectations for student, for teacher, and for the school administrator are quite different. . . . In effect, persons occupying a given position are expected to fulfill, within a range, their group's slowly changing expectations for this position."[3]

Zander says, "In its most general sense a role is a set of behaviors which an individual is expected to perform. The more restricted meaning we have given the term is that a professional role includes a limited set of behaviors concerning, for example, task functions, responsibility relations, and normative relationships which are expected of an individual by relevant others. These expectations of a role occupant may be called prescriptions for the role. . . . Task functions are the work contributions he is expected to make while a member of that role. . . . Responsibility relations specify what degree of authority he has over others or what accountability he may expect from them, as well as how much authority others have over him and the accountability he has to them. When one participates in a given task function, it is usually stated explicitly or implicitly that he is to have contacts with designated other persons in fulfilling this obligation. . . . Whatever the duty, once a person assumes a given function there are concomitant expectations as to how he is to relate himself to specified others. . . . A person occupying a particular role often has specific beliefs prescribed for him which concern the nature of his relationships with other persons. These prescribed evaluations are distinct from responsibility relations. Though an accurate label is difficult to select, they will be called normative relationships. They may concern evaluations a role occupant is expected to make about himself, in comparison to those in other roles on, for example, his comparative knowledge, skill, or training."[4]

Boehm offers this succinct definition, "Role, then describes the activities and tasks which an individual is expected to perform by virtue of his membership in social groups and his participation in social institutions. . . . Role expectation refers to the activities considered appropriate for the role in the light of social norms which prescribe role behavior. . . . Role perception refers to the way role is viewed, either by the person performing the role or by the reciprocal person."[5]

Executives and agency presidents usually use the word role to mean *activities* and *tasks*. Doing so they must answer the following questions: What activities and tasks is the executive expected to perform in his work with the board? What activities and tasks *is* the president expected to perform?

It is important for these administrative leaders to state

the basic assumptions which underlie their definitions of role.

First, the administrative leader's role is a reflection of his personal philosophy and his philosophy of administration. If his philosophy of administration is based on the concepts of "enabling" and "leadership" then he must see his job as one of helping groups to do their work, and in addition, he is responsible for influencing the board in all matters where basic principles are required as a foundation for decisions.

Second, the administrative leader's role is dynamic and always depends upon a variety of factors, including the different and changing needs of the board and the changing situation in the agency and community.

Third, despite the dynamic nature of the role and the variables that are present in particular situations, there are certain task functions that are performed in some degree by all administrative leaders at certain times.

Fourth, many of the task functions are shared by the president and the executive, so there must be a clear definition of who does what.

Where there are shared responsibilities the importance of good relationships and of clearly defined roles and responsibilities cannot be overstressed. This point is illustrated by these excerpts from records kept by executive directors:

"The executive director reviewed and revised material prepared by the president on their roles and that of the outside consultant who would help with this project, to insure clarity and proper assignment of responsibilities. The president and the center chairman agreed on procedures. When additional persons were suggested for the committee, the president would make the appointments."

Responsibilities should be defined in relation to the evolving situation:

"During a lengthy telephone conversation with the president about development in the West area, we decided that I, as executive director, would attend the organization meeting to get information on ideas and plans of other agencies. This talk gave us an opportunity to clarify our next steps and responsibilities."

An executive points out what may happen when roles are not thought through in a long-range fashion: "My chairman and I tend to focus on the next piece of work to be completed. I feel this has disadvantages. We're spending too much time on mechanics; we should be spending more time on the over-all design."

Since role means a set of tasks which the person is expected to perform in a defined situation, to establish the general role of the administrative volunteer one must also establish the role of the professional worker.

Admitting the fact that there are many variables of agency size, situation, community condition, purposes, and the like, nevertheless, the professional worker has the role of enabling or helping the board or committee to arrive at the best possible decisions. In his discussion of common elements in administration Thompson accents the vital role of the executive in work with the board when he says: "We know that often the chief executive is the key member of such a group and that when the board or council does effectively discharge organization-directing responsibilities this fact frequently reflects *the chief execu-tive's capacity to energize his board or council.* . . . To operate effectively the chief executive must play an im-portant part in the organization directing function."[6]

In addition, the executive is responsible for guiding the efforts of the staff members who are working with him. This includes the definition of each person's responsibility and the continuing process of helping them fulfill their responsibilities. Work with staff is described in the next chapter.

In the day-to-day job, it is important that the executive and staff be responsible for making decisions relative to the procedures and programs needed to carry out the policies and purposes of the agency. In addition to being responsible for understanding the job to which he is assigned, the professional worker must continuously con-sult with other workers in his field so that he will keep abreast of new knowledge and the most effective ways of rendering service.

Administrative volunteers are ordinarily thought of as the major policy-making group. They may be appointed or elected to work with others to advance the program of the agency. They must make policy decisions regarding purpose, program, personnel, finance, and public relations. They bring to the agency general experience rather than specific professional education. This general experience enables them to study and interpret community needs. They must know the history, purpose, and prevailing policies, programs, and procedures of the agency. Since the administrative volunteer is responsible for major policy decisions, he must also seek constantly to evaluate the work of the agency so that there may be certainty that these policies are sound.

More and more, it is evident that professional workers and administrative volunteers must see the relationship of the job they do, however small, to the total effort of the agency. In addition, they must be helped to feel and understand the importance of their specific contribution. Furthermore, they must have planned opportunities for growth, learning, and development. They must establish good working relationships and must behave responsibly toward one another as they fulfill their specific commitments to the total enterprise.[7]

Along this line an agency president commented:

"As the executive and I work together longer we find that we spend more time discussing total agency problems. This is probably because we know each other better, approach problems similarly, and have a deep-seated concern for the total."

In the next excerpt we see the president and the executive director going out to learn firsthand about an important part of the total agency:

"This evening the executive and I went to the Northeast Branch Committee of Management meeting. We try to cover branch meetings and attended this one because program and personnel as circumscribed by budget were to be considered. There was sensible but spirited talk about the service we do give in the area and what we ought to give; the people we do reach and those we should. There seemed to be no hostility to 'those people at Metropolitan.' The program chairman made an excellent presentation. The executive and I did not speak much during the meeting. It was not necessary to do so."

The national and world aspects of the YWCA are recognized by this president:

"I went to a national support meeting at the home of a board member. Talked world YWCA program to a great many people at lunch. This seems to be an important part of my job."

Leadership of Boards and Committees

What are some of the things executives and presidents must do if boards and committees are to be more effective? Among the many things that could be listed the following represent some of the more important ones.

1. They must help boards and committees to choose effective members.

2. They must help boards and committees to define their purposes and objectives.

3. They must help boards and committees to organize for effective work.

4. They must help boards and committees to learn how to work within the policies of the particular agency.

5. They must help boards and committees to develop good procedures and good methods of work.

6. They must help boards and committees learn to work within the community setting.

7. They must help individuals to develop their skill, as is illustrated by the following material written by an executive:

"Agenda conference with Mrs. H, the chairman. She never thinks about the committee until we meet in agenda conferences! Much planning must be done with her so that she sees her role as something more than only the presiding officer of the group. I am trying to get her to initiate suggestions now and then but this will require time and effort on my part."

(Later comment from executive who has observed how Mrs. H has changed.)

"Mrs. H has gone out of her way to involve herself in the discussions. This is a new role—her seeking and finding ways in which she can contribute. I suspect in Mrs. H's case at first she did not have the skill or confidence she needed. She now finds herself more comfortable and she has developed her skills." The professional worker has been good about helping Mrs. H become more skilled.

8. They must understand that it is important for them to help build good social relationships between the members of task groups. They should see to it that persons know one another, know why they are there as individuals and know what their role is. Administrative leaders should understand also that it takes time to establish this cohesiveness. At the beginning of the group's experience there will be a period of "feeling out" and adjusting to one another until individuals feel secure. Throughout the experience

with the task group administrative leaders must concentrate on helping the individuals developing
shared values and purposes. They do this by the
continuous statement and restatement of fundamental purposes and by the use of examples as they
formulate and reformulate the goals. Another aspect
of working with the task group is helping them develop a pace of work which will be rapid enough to
bring the satisfaction of achievement but not so fast
as to be overwhelming. An executive underlines the
importance of helping groups develop their cohesiveness if they are to become productive: "Cohesiveness, rapport, relationships have to be considered first in any group, before it can become
productive. I had thought that the committee was
more ready to get to its job than it really was. As
individuals they all recognized the problem and
wanted to work on it. But certain groundwork had
to be done before any progress could be noted.
People had to learn how to work with one another."

9. They must help individual members learn how to
carry their assignments.

10. They must help boards and committees understand
and evaluate their own work. In the area of evaluation an executive reports:

"The president and I evaluated the work we had
done this far and took another look at our time
schedule. We wanted to counteract any feeling on
the part of the group that there was great pressure
to get the assignment done. We were approaching

a crucial part and we would hate to see the group rush through for the sake of meeting a date. This phase required time to arrive at carefully thought-out conclusions and recommendations."

11. Perhaps the greatest responsibility of administrative leaders is to help boards and committees organize their work in relation to a clear set of purposes and goals. This means that they must be skillful in distinguishing between immediate and short-range goals and long-range basic purposes. Here they must take sufficient time in working with people to help them reach understanding and consensus as to the major objective of their efforts.

12. In addition, they must help the many committees see their work in relation to all of the work that is being carried on by other committees and groups in the agency. In other words, they must organize their tasks with a comprehension of the total job that is being done by the agency. Few people have exactly the same comprehension of the agency as a whole because wholeness implies vision and looking ahead and it is known that situations look different to different people who view them from a variety of points of vantage and experience. The executive and the president must help people to see the total job of the agency, as is pointed out below:

"The president and the executive director discussed in advance the first meeting of the board. We went over our roles at the meeting, and the assignment of tasks. We did this to be sure the agenda was understood and that the mechanics of the meeting were arranged, and that our roles were clear. Later we met to go over the agenda in detail. It included explanations of various committees and their functions and the calendar for the year to be approved by the board. I felt some explanation of the relationship between committee chairmen was important at this point. I was aware that the president was relatively new and was not entirely clear about metropolitan relationships. So we took plenty of time to go over every item."

13. Furthermore, administrative leaders must help boards and committees organize their tasks with a special regard for priority and an arrangement of jobs in terms of significance and importance. This calls for a reconciliation of several variables; the task to be done in relation to a large number of tasks, the time and timing factors, the importance of the specific in relation to the over-all design of the whole. Perhaps it is fair to say that every board and committee have more jobs than can ever be done. Consequently administrative leaders must help groups make choices in relation to which job is most important at the moment.

14. Another responsibility is to help the board and committee to organize the work to be done into manageable units so that a sense of productivity is forthcoming without excessive delay. This kind of division of labor must then be followed by regular

171

attention to co-ordination and the relating of the various parts.

15. Another responsibility is to provide a channel of communication between the various work groups and between the various work-group leaders. Here, the administrative leader fulfills the role of an integrator or a person able to facilitate the growing unity of the agency.

16. One of the most important responsibilities of the administrative leader is to help boards and committees organize their work so that there is a systematic arrangement of tasks in relation to the capacities and capabilities of the board and committee members. Boards need jobs that are challenging to them, but at the same time they should not be asked to take jobs that will be overwhelming to them. As Johns has put it, "Helping the board of directors and committees of an organization is a professional skill of the highest order. It is one of the key lay-professional relationships. The staff service provided is one of the critical factors in determining board and committee effectiveness. Executives and other staff members can assist the board and the organization's committees in a number of ways: they can help in the wise selection of board and committee personnel; they can help to clarify the assignments given to committees; they can help to develop agendas which aid boards to get their work done; they can help get the in-between meeting work done; they can help the president or com-

mittee chairman to develop skill in getting participation."[8]

In a recent study conducted by the author,[9] the duties of the executive in working with the board were summarized in the following propositions:

PROPOSITION 1. *The executive has a role in board and committee formulation and composition.* Tasks may include suggesting persons for nomination or appointment, obtaining background data on prospective persons, making contact with prospective persons to discuss the assignment and assess the degree of interest, suggesting needs for new committees or expansion of old committees, suggesting the size committees should be, suggesting the frequency of committee meetings, suggesting persons for the chairmanship, reviewing board and committee composition, suggesting discontinuance of committees no longer needed.

PROPOSITION 2. *The executive has a role in working with individual board and committee members,* especially the president and committee chairman, to help them to perform their jobs. Tasks may include: providing information and background material; providing personal and professional opinion and judgment; helping them to understand their duties and to plan their work; helping with orientation and education; stimulating, motivating, and encouraging participation; focusing effort on the most important issues; helping resolve conflicts; helping individuals develop their leadership capacities. In the excerpt which follows, a clear division of responsibilities between the executive and president is described:

"We spent time going over the things that we have done

173

as a team. We noted that we have not always done things together. We started off together and still talk things over and then take our individual assignments. Division of responsibility has fallen more or less like this. President has contacts with volunteers. She has worked with chairmen in calling and setting up meetings. She has made all arrangements with volunteers. Executive has prepared materials, worked with the president more as a resource, interpreting and filling in on history, policies, and background. Looking at the whole job we felt our biggest contribution was at the point of interpretation of the total agency."

PROPOSITION 3. *The executive has a role in working with the board or committee as a group to help it perform its assigned responsibilities.* Tasks may include: helping with agenda preparation; presenting material on professional concepts, principles, and trends; participating in policy discussions; helping in budget planning and control; suggesting work methods and procedures; summarizing material; directing methods of evaluating performance; suggesting what is involved in implementing plans; interpreting and clarifying agency purpose and function; co-ordinating the work of committees with the total agency program; clarifying the function of the board or committee and setting limits on its work; presenting reports of agency programs and problems; providing studies and providing facts; stimulating the examination of policies and of program in the light of community needs and attitudes.

The executive is helpful in reviewing and summarizing board or committee discussion, as is noted in this example:

"Once during the meeting, of my own accord I reviewed some of the points that seemed like conclusions. I did this to get members of the group to consider what they had said and to see what had been omitted and what more needed to be done. Twice later the chairman asked me again to summarize the conclusions the group seemed to have arrived at. My role seems to be shaping up along these lines."

PROPOSITION 4. *The executive has a responsibility to function as a liaison worker between the various groups.* Tasks may include: presenting staff thinking, experience, and concerns to the board or vice versa; presenting and interpreting board action to the staff or staff action to the board; carrying out agency policy established by the board; working with some staff members who have board or committee assignments; providing appropriate channels of communication between board and staff and community groups; co-ordinating the board and staff and other groups to form a unified agency.

PROPOSITION 5. *The executive has the responsibility of carrying a liaison role between the board or committee and the community.* Tasks may include: interpreting board policies and actions to the community; interpreting community needs, attitudes, and resources to the board and helping them relate agency goals to changing community needs; collecting, preparing, and presenting community data needed for program and policy decisions; working with the board to develop a public relations program; interpreting the programs of other agencies in the field of service and presenting them.

The five propositions presented above may be used as

a basis for deciding that certain tasks may be assumed by the president in certain situations. For example, in the large cities it has been noted that agency presidents are often expected to carry extensive planning responsibilities. As the chief administrative volunteer, the president may represent the agency in large interagency undertakings.

Work with Members or Constituency

Administrative leaders always have some kind of relationships with the membership, clientele, or constituency of the agency. If they believe administrative policies and practices should receive critical evaluation from the constituency as an essential means of checking on and improving the work, they must provide the avenues for constituents to give it. Constituency or member groups must be made to feel their important role in the agency. To be sure, there are differences in the ways community service agencies will relate to constituency groups. Some agencies, such as the YWCA, are membership organizations, wherein the constituency is the agency. In such an agency, administrative relationships with members of various classifications and with electors have been studied in considerable detail.[10] In other agencies persons relate as individuals and there is a service basis rather than a membership basis.

Various terms are used to describe the persons served by the community agency or participating in its program. Some speak of their clients or clientele; others refer to members or their membership; some refer to their constituents or constituency. A client is a person who seeks professional advice and service from another person. Thus a clientele is a body of clients. But generally speaking there is little of the group aspect one associates with membership. Members belong to an association or organization. They are individuals who join or affiliate with one another and in so doing accept the purpose of the association. Constituency refers to the body of persons related to the agency or potentially to be related to it at the point of membership participation, receipt of professional service, or general support of the agency. Constituency is a broad term which is used to designate any and all of the persons who benefit from the service or program aspect of the agency.

There is increasing evidence to support the fact that the constituency of the community service agency has a function beyond that of merely accepting services. The constituency has a place to play in the total administrative process of the agency. Among the many things constituency can do are these: *First,* constituency can be very active in helping the agency understand the community needs which must be met; *second,* constituency can give expression regarding the kinds of programs or services that are most likely to aid in the meeting of these needs; *third,* constituency can function at the vital point of policy determination; *fourth,* constituency can be a potent resource for agency interpretation and support; *fifth,* constituency can assist the agency in evaluating the quality of its work and can suggest modifications and improvements.

In his discussion of administration as a system of responsibility Sayre asks the questions, "To whom is the organization accountable? For what is the organization accountable? How is this accountability defined and by

whom? How is this accountability judged and by whom?
. . . Administration as a system of responsibility is concerned with identifying, defining, clarifying, and carrying
out the organization's relationship with its relevant external environment. It is concerned with the way in which
the organization reports on its plans and its accomplishments to its constituency and secures the judgment and
evaluation of that constituency. . . . *The term constituency is central.* The organization serves not itself but a
constituency or, more likely, a number of constituencies.
In any organization the price of survival is sensitivity to
the requirements of its constituencies. What are these constituencies? What is the relationship and responsibility of
the organization to each of these constituencies; and by
whom and how are these constituencies, these relationships
and responsibilities, to be defined? Reporting to these
constituencies in relevant and significant terms is a second
concern of this conceptual system. And providing adequate
opportunities for the constituencies to communicate their
appraisal of the organization in a meaningful context with
some assurance of being listened to by the decision makers
of the organization is a third concern. These three roads
lead to an end product which is the major value or premise
of the conceptual system: namely, that an organization requires for its survival, in a state of health, a system of responsibility, a method of assuring that it is actually, not
merely ritualistically, accountable to those who create it,
support or are served by the organization."[11]

In many agencies members are elected to serve on important committees or the board of the agency. Frequently
agencies hold membership meetings or hearings on impor-

tant matters of policy decision. Informal surveys of member opinion are constantly available if the agency staff who render direct services are alert to their opportunities. Well-prepared bulletins and other forms of written material can do much to create a co-operative relationship between leadership and membership.

The first characteristic of a good relationship between administration and constituency is that it be consciously sought and desired, systematically studied and developed, and thoughtfully guided. Furthermore, when relationships are good the channels of communication are free and open. Administrators and constituents have access to one another. Communication and accessibility are essential if there is to be any kind of effective co-operation. There must be regular sharing of information and experience, and a maximum of working together which minimizes the emphasis formerly put on "we," the administrators, and "they," the constituents. Instead of isolation from one another every opportunity for joint work should be utilized as a means of strengthening the total agency. In addition, when deliberate attempts are made to strengthen the ties of relationship between constituency and administration, staff responsibility for work with the constituency is spread out, distributed, decentralized throughout the entire agency.

In the next chapter executive leadership responsibility with staff will be discussed.

NOTES

1. Nathan E. Cohen, *The Citizen Volunteer* (New York, N.Y.: Harper & Brothers, 1960), p. 33.

2. Arthur Blumberg and Seth Arsenian, "A Deeper Look at Volunteers," *Adult Leadership*, June, 1960.

3. Henry Maas, "Concepts and Methods in Social Work Research," *New Directions in Social Work*, ed. Cora Kasins (New York, N.Y.: Harper & Brothers, 1954), pp. 229–230.

4. Alvin Zander, Arthur R. Cohen, and Ezra Stotland, *Role Relations in the Mental Health Professions* (Ann Arbor, Mich.: University of Michigan, Research Center for Group Dynamics, Institute for Social Research, 1957), pp. 15–17.

5. Werner W. Boehm, *The Social Casework Method in Social Work Education* (New York, N.Y.: Council on Social Work Education, 1959), pp. 97–100.

6. James Thompson, "Common Elements in the Emerging Profession of Administration." A report by The Pittsburgh Area "Committee on Common Elements in Administration," sponsored by the National Conference on Social Welfare. Presented at Atlantic City, June 6, 1960.

7. Harleigh B. Trecker, "The Role of the Professional Worker in the Volunteer Agency," *The Newsletter*, Girl Scouts of U.S.A., New York, May, 1958.

8. Ray Johns, *Executive Responsibility* (New York, N.Y.: Association Press, 1954), p. 73.

9. Harleigh B. Trecker, *Executive Role with Boards—An Exploratory Study* (University of Connecticut, School of Social Work, 1960).

10. *Membership Practices in Community YWCAs* (New York, N.Y.: National Board, YWCA, 1960).

11. Wallace Sayre, "Some General Observations on the Principles of Administration." Presented at Conference of Association of University Programs in Hospital Administration, Lake Shore Club, Chicago, December 27–30, 1954.

CHAPTER **9**

Work with Staff

I N THE previous chapter attention was centered on
work with the board, committees, and members. Much
of that material has pertinence for work with the staff as
well. However, inasmuch as the executive as "chief-of-
staff" has the over-all responsibility for providing leadership for his fellow workers, special aspects of staff administration will be stressed in this discussion. Executives
must know how to help staffs to develop responsible work
patterns and processes. They must provide the conditions
in the agency setting which will make for organized productive effort on the part of the total staff. Capable executive leadership is essential if the staff is to be expected to
perform to the best of its ability. The staff needs this leadership and usually seeks it.

Effective Executives

What kind of executives seem to be most effective in helping staff to get work done?

First, they accept staff as having personal worth, dignity, and capacity to do their assigned jobs.

Second, they are themselves enthusiastic and vigorous in their approach to their work.

Third, they are confident that the work can and will be done at a high level of achievement.

Fourth, they provide an atmosphere or climate which is essentially warm, friendly, and relaxed.

Fifth, they are available for consultation when it is needed.

Sixth, they are basically supportive, positive, and constructive in the consultation that they give.

Seventh, they give general rather than close and detailed supervision.

Eighth, they help to outline general procedures and then encourage the staff to use their experience and intelligence in getting their jobs done.

Ninth, they encourage staff to participate in setting goals for the agency's work because it is known that there is a relationship between participation in goal setting and work accomplishment.

McGregor sums it up when he says "The characteristics of daily behavior and attitudes to which subordinates respond with sensitivity do not spring from the air. They are manifestations of the superior's conception of the managerial job and his assumptions about human nature. . . .

The manager who holds persons in high esteem has a relatively high opinion of the intelligence and capacity of the average human being. He may well be aware that he is endowed with substantial capacity, but he does not perceive himself as a member of a limited elite. He sees most human beings as having real capacity for growth and development, for the acceptance of responsibility, for creative accomplishment. He regards his subordinates as genuine assets in helping him fulfill his own responsibilities, and he is concerned with creating the conditions which enable him to realize these assets."[1]

Effective Staffs

What conditions underlie successful, effective staff productivity? Administrative leaders must understand that productive work does not just happen. They must be familiar with the conditions which seem to be necessary if work groups are to accomplish their tasks. Many studies from a variety of fields enable us to single out certain conditions which seem to be essential.

First, staffs produce more when they are composed or made up of the right people. That is, they have people qualified in terms of competence, skill, and ability, to do the assigned job.

Two, productive staff members have assignments which are within the realm of their competence.

Three, they are clear on the over-all purpose or goal they are trying to achieve. They are straight on their assignments from the start.

Four, productive staff groups have good advance, over-all planning and preparation.

Five, productive staff groups think through the methods they will use in carrying through on their assignment.

Six, productive staff groups divide their total assignment into parts and take one step at a time as they proceed with their work.

Seven, they develop a time schedule and work within a time framework. In so far as possible they relate specific work goals to this time schedule.

Eight, productive staff groups have good leadership or chairmanship, able to release thinking, focus discussion, and bring the group along to decisions.

Nine, they make periodic assessments of what they have accomplished and what are the next steps.

Ten, they are given appropriate recognition for their accomplishments as a way of building and sustaining pride in their work.

According to McGregor, "The accumulation of knowledge about human behavior in many specialized fields has made possible the formulation of a number of generalizations which provide a modest beginning for a new theory with respect to the management of human resources. Some of the assumptions of this new theory are:

1. The expenditure of mental and physical effort in work is as natural as play or rest . . .

2. Man will exercise self-direction and self-control in the service of objectives to which he is committed.

3. Commitment to objectives is a function of the rewards associated with their achievement. The most significant of such rewards, that is, the satisfaction of ego and

self-actualization needs, can be direct products of effort directed toward organizational objectives.

4. The average human being learns, under proper conditions, not only to accept but to seek responsibility.

5. The capacity to exercise a relatively high degree of imagination, ingenuity, and creativity in the solution of organizational problems is widely, not narrowly, distributed in the population.

6. Under the conditions of modern industrial life, the intellectual potentialities of the average human being are only partially utilized."[2]

Personnel Administration

The executive must assume major responsibility for sound personnel practices. While he may delegate certain aspects of this work he must have an over-all grasp of sound personnel theory. Many agencies have documented their standards of personnel administration. In 1958 the National YWCA published a revised personnel administration manual. In this very important tool document they state, "The strength of the entire YWCA movement today depends primarily on the quality of its leadership and on the extent to which it is able to employ and retain competent, devoted, and satisfied personnel for its professional positions."

The manual goes on to say, "in order that the YWCA may, in the face of womanpower shortage, secure and retain staff to fulfill its obligations to the community, the recruiting of professional staff should become a concerted program of major importance, with countrywide involvement of staff and volunteers."

The report then goes on to spell out basic YWCA personnel policies and practices. The following words are used:

"1. Employment standards—maintain YWCA minimum requirements for employment, hiring only those with the educational background and capacities necessary for the assumption of professional responsibilities.

"2. Training—provide adequate training for professional workers through a diversified program on many levels, with special provisions for training mature persons re-entering the labor market.

"3. Use of staff—experiment with: flexible scheduling, better use of experienced staff, qualified part-time workers, short-term specialists, and interrupted career women. Make choices of program and services since the YWCA cannot be 'all things to all people.'

"4. Salaries—review salary ranges and wage scales periodically and adjust them as circumstances require. Salaries and wages should compare favorably with those paid by business, industry, government, schools, health and welfare agencies, for comparable education, experience and potentialities for development on the job. Salaries must be high enough to enable staff to (a) enjoy a decent standard of living (b) develop their personal and professional potential through graduate study, membership in professional organizations, and participation in a variety of cultural activities."

In an excellent statement the manual spells out the principles of personnel administration in the YWCA as follows: "to simplify personnel administration, the personnel responsibilities of the board, personnel committee, personnel chairman, executive director, and supervisory staff should be clearly defined, recorded, and assigned.

"1. Employment procedures—the board of directors, on authority vested in it by the electorate, employs the executive director, who in turn is responsible, in consultation with the personnel chairman, for selecting and engaging staff.

"2. Letter of employment—it is recommended that YWCAs use, when new staff members are engaged, an official letter of employment rather than annual contracts. In the opinion of many YWCA boards and staffs and most other welfare and health agencies, an indeterminate period of employment seems to have advantages over the annual contract as a device to reduce turnover.

"3. Supervision and performance evaluation—the executive director as head of staff is vested by the board of directors with the responsibility for seeing that other employees of the association are assigned, trained, and supervised and their job performances evaluated. The continuing supervisory covers all aspects of the worker's job performance in relation to members, volunteer and work leaders, staff, committees, board of directors, and the community. The supervisor is responsible for keeping up to date, through appropriate consultation, on all these aspects of performance, and for sharing pertinent information with the worker. She is responsible for continuing evaluation of performance in regularly scheduled supervisory conferences and for periodic written summary evaluations which must reflect the judgments of supervisor, supervisee, and the related chairman or other volunteer. The written evaluation helps to maintain a high level of supervision, and consequently contributes to the quality of service to the community."

Along this same line, in a nationally used publication entitled *Guide for Agency Self Appraisal,* the author listed the following criteria of professional personnel practices: "An effective agency is staffed by a sufficient number of qualified personnel to provide leadership and services focused upon the attainment of the goals of the agency. It has a comprehensive program of supervision aimed at the continuous improvement of worker performance. Among the criteria are:

1. The agency has a clearly written statement of personnel policies and practices.

2. The agency has an active personnel committee.

3. Staff members are represented on the personnel committee.

4. The agency has carefully developed procedures for selecting, employing, and orienting new staff members.

5. The agency has written job descriptions including the duties and responsibilities of each staff member.

6. The agency seeks to employ professional staff professional members qualified in terms of training, competence, and experience. The agency has a regular written staff evaluation procedure.

7. The agency is fully staffed.

8. The agency has a plan and a program for staff advancement.

9. The agency makes periodic reviews of its personnel policies, procedures, and practices.

10. The agency has a written statement covering its program of supervision for the staff.

11. The agency has an adequate number of trained supervisory personnel to provide staff supervision.

12. The agency has developed a comprehensive program of staff supervision.

13. The agency has a program of in-service training.

14. The agency has regular staff meetings.

15. The agency supervisors have regular individual conferences with staff members.

16. The agency has a library of periodicals and books related to its field of work.

17. The agency has an educational leave policy so that staff members may secure further training.

18. The agency has a policy with reference to staff participation in conferences, institutes, and other professional learning opportunities.

19. The agency has an adequate retirement plan for employees."

Steps in Personnel Planning

In modern personnel planning and administration certain steps are required.

First, the agency must determine and classify the total work required to carry out the program within the framework of designated objectives and policies.

Second, the agency must classify the total work into primary constituent kinds of work: that is, program, business management, administration, and so forth.

Third, the agency must divide the work as so classified into manageable components, positions, or jobs.

Fourth, the agency must group like jobs together into an orderly pattern of organization or structure.

Fifth, the agency must define salary and wage policies for all positions.

Sixth, the agency must define responsibility and accountability lines and relationships for each position, and must spell out the relationships between positions.

Seventh, the agency must establish supervisory controls and relationships and develop a program of supervision.

Eighth, the agency must organize time schedules for all workers on weekly, monthly, and annual basis.

Ninth, the agency must develop a system of intercommunication and co-operation so that all workers will engage themselves as team members.

Tenth, the agency must develop a plan for appraising, measuring, and readjusting work loads in relation to evolving standards and changing circumstances.

Every large organization must have a comprehensive personnel development program designed to secure and maintain an effective and purposeful staff. Elements in this personnel development program include procedures for performance analysis and appraisal, an individual study program for each staff member, sound processes of induction and orientation, thoughtfully conceived in-service training opportunities, regular staff meetings, and a strong program of supervision. Supervision refers to the continuous direction, guidance, and ongoing help for staff members in a one-to-one relationship. It requires regularly scheduled supervisory conferences, periodic evaluation of work, and an annual performance appraisal.

In discussing the characteristics of good personnel organization Urice mentions ten points which represent a good summary. He calls for proper divisions of work, effective co-ordination of work and workers, clear definitions of responsibilities and relationships, authority which is established and defined in a manner that leaves no uncertainty, single lines of responsibility and accountability, sufficient decentralization with thinking and planning done as near as possible to the points of responsibility for performance, a manageable span of control, adequate communication, adequate standard practices, and adequate records.[3]

Executive Assistance in Work Organization

What are some of the ways executives may help individual staff members and staff groups learn how to organize their work?

First, they may help at the point of definition of individual and group tasks so that persons involved will be clear as to their specific responsibility.

Second, they may help by discussing and determining upon starting points for definite projects when a variety of starting points present themselves.

Third, they may help at the point of scheduling or projecting a time schedule so that persons will know when assignments must be completed to make their work coincide with the work of others.

Fourth, they may be helpful in drafting a written plan of work for a given individual or department. Sometimes a broad outline with regard to a particular project helps provide an organized framework within which to proceed.

Fifth, they may help by bringing together two or more groups or individuals who are sharing responsibility for a particular project.

Sixth, they may be helpful by encouraging staff committees to limit themselves by realistically defining their objectives and working toward goals which are distinctly within the realm of possibility.

Seventh, through over-all agency surveys and studies it is possible to help the staff evaluate the degree of organization attained and what modifications should be made.

Administrative leaders have several means at their disposal as they endeavor to help individuals and groups learn how to organize their work. In individual conferences with staff members, it is possible to dwell upon organizational aspects of their respective tasks. In group meetings of the staff it is desirable to focus attention on work organization. The continuous program of agency education can allow for more formal discussion of this problem. By means of reports, prepared materials, and study outlines it is frequently possible to center attention on the criteria of good organization. In periodic evaluation conferences this aspect of the work may be considered.

Personal Work Organization

In outlining the personal qualifications needed by executives Dimock places considerable stress on "orderliness, stability, and consistency in mental processes and workmanship. . . . The importance of a mind that functions in a consecutive and orderly way in the management aspect of administration is so apparent that it hardly calls for elaboration. What is not so readily recognized is that the moral and spiritual order of the association is rooted in and dependent upon the orderliness, consistency, and dependability of the chief executive. Disorder of mind and habit at the center of the organization generates disorder; caprice breeds chaos, but order begets order."[4]

Practically every executive is faced with the problem of personal work organization. Administrators know that the way they organize their work has an influence on the total agency. If their work patterns and processes are soundly and thoughtfully developed they set a tone for the entire enterprise.

From observing and talking with a considerable number of executives it is possible to summarize some of the suggestions they offer with reference to personal work organization. Executives who are well organized and productive in their own pursuits seem to do at least some of the following:

1. They maintain a carefully planned schedule and calendar of activities.

2. They regularize as many things as possible, doing them at the same time each day or each week.

3. They choose tasks in relation to their readiness and their mood and time available.

4. They make use of brief periods of time, including the ten minutes or fifteen minutes.

5. They try to work ahead of schedule at least a little bit to avoid pressure of last-minute work.

6. They try to carry through on a task rather than drop it and start several other tasks.

7. They develop a system of files and tools, and know where the things are that they need.

8. They ask themselves frequently whether or not it would be possible to delegate an assignment to someone else who could do it better and more rapidly.

9. For big jobs they develop an outline or plan of approach.

10. They take free periods to refresh themselves.

11. They keep a time record now and then to see where their time goes and how they might budget their time better.

The Importance of Purposes

In the creating of an organized work environment purposes are of central importance. Executives must help the staff to understand the purposes for their particular tasks in relationship to the purpose of the agency as a whole. Unless work groups have purposes which are clearly stated, leadership is difficult. Furthermore it is hard to co-ordinate the work of the specific group with that of others. In addition the motivation of the staff is likely to be low and it is difficult to challenge them to their best performance. It is also known that unless purposes are clearly stated it is next to impossible to evaluate the work of the staff. A staff member may work many weeks or months without having any feeling of accomplishment because he has not clearly understood what his goals are. In general, it might be stated that the product of staff meetings improves when care and attention is given to spelling out the basic purposes which the group is trying to achieve. If purposes are clear perhaps complaints such as the following can be eliminated or at least reduced.

A state child welfare administrator asks, "Can't we cut down first a little more on voluminous recording, endless conferencing and consulting? At least, must we all attend every conference? The conferencing, which makes me very uneasy, is the kind, on one case situation, between two agencies, two workers, two supervisors, two supervisors' supervisors, and occasionally, two agency executives. Can you see a doctor saying, 'My days are taken up with conferences with other doctors, pathologists, anesthetists, nurses, and hospital administrators. My evenings and my colleagues' evenings are taken up with writing reports on all these conferences, so I will be able to serve only 10 of the 300 patients needing my service'?"[5]

Purpose is important in agency budget decisions:

"Later in the day we discussed the public relations aspect of the agency's budget conference with the United Fund. It is necessary that we tell the story properly and focus on the distinctive purpose and contribution of our work."

It is important in relation to staff selection:

"A definite personal commitment is needed in order to function effectively in our agency. It is not just another agency. Sometimes in selecting workers one is deceived about the amount of commitment of an individual. To some, new vistas are opened, and one sees the growth process unfold. In others there is no such challenge."

It must be emphasized in training institutes:

"The need for basic information on the purpose of the agency and its methods of work was emphasized, and the staff committee asked the executive director to give such information. The role of the executive was that of interpreting need, correlating staff and volunteer ideas and interests, and guiding the planning for the total enterprise.

Even with long-time agency members it is necessary to review the fundamentals of purpose and methods:

"It is simply amazing how individuals can be exposed to things over a long period of time and never really hear and understand what has been going on around them. As all of the staff members are outstanding professionals it was assumed they had a certain background of knowledge or frame of reference. They did have some knowledge, but it was slanted from their particular vantage point. So as the group proceeded it was continuously necessary to review how certain things came to be the way they are and to interpret the purpose of the agency and how it functions."

Purposes are definitely related to staff morale. Roy says: "Morale may be defined as the degree to which organization goals and goals of the individuals who comprise organization are compatible, to such extent as those goals have common ground. . . . Good morale requires the individual pursuit of organization goals with enthusiasm and energy. . . . Good morale further requires the individuals in organization to pursue organization goals with energy that is supplied voluntarily, because they want to as individuals, not because it is the wish of the 'boss' or through threat of punishment or promise of reward."[6]

March and Simon stressed the importance of time and timing when they asked and answered a question, "What determines the type of activity that members of an organization will engage in? First, the greater the explicit time pressure attached to an activity, the greater the propensity to engage in it. The stimulus of deadlines tends to direct attention to some tasks rather than to others. Second, the greater the clarity of goals associated with an activity, the greater the propensity to engage in it."[7]

Executives have a real responsibility to think through the questions of time and timing and to help their staff to do likewise. Copeland makes the observation:

"Timing is an art. Although proficiency in timing unquestionably can be improved by study and practice, I suspect that a sense of timing at least comes close to being an innate quality. . . . In most business decisions timing is an element; there is a question not only as to what to do but also as to when to do it; and nicety in timing is a deft achievement. . . . The time span . . . within which action has to be taken to attain its maximum effectiveness . . . varies with every situation. In some cases plenty of time is available for working out plans and putting them into effect. In many other cases the executive and his staff have to 'work against time,' that is, the span is so uncomfortably limited that preparations have to be compressed into a short period and short cuts have to be taken wherever possible. . . . Part of the art of timing lies in an executive's ability to read the handwriting on the wall or otherwise to sense an impending change well in advance of the point where it mounts to full force. The executive who has such a knack usually enjoys a relatively long time span within which to prepare for dealing with a new situation. . . . Foresight in anticipating administrative problems provides a longer time for action and thereby not only permits more careful preparation but also allows greater freedom of action. Conversely, a lack of foresight leads to handicaps. . . . Foresight becomes conspicuous through its absence, and the greater the lack of foresight, the less the freedom in planning of one's actions."[8]

The element of timing is brought out in the following excerpts:

"We are under continuing pressure to cut down on the number of staff and committee meetings. The president wondered if it wouldn't be better to have monthly or even quarterly meetings of the staff. I tried to make clear how our present timing gives us more time in the long run."

"Some of the staff members seemed to be unhappy to think that we could not finish our task tonight. I referred back to what we were trying to accomplish and said that I thought that it was more important for us to come up with sound, well thought out recommendations than to rush our thinking to meet a deadline. I emphasized the fact that we were planning for the future development of a vast geographic area and I thought it important that we do this carefully and thoughtfully."

After a lengthy budget discussion the executive director said, "Although after about six hours of discussion with break for lunch we were mentally and physically exhausted, I thought we achieved a deeper level of insight and analysis than we could have if we made another date to finish up the job."

Work with Staff Committees

More and more large agencies make use of staff committees to plan and carry through major pieces of work. These committees need special consideration and help from agency executives.

The following list of questions can be used by the executive in conference with a committee chairman:

1. What is the assignment to the committee? What is it supposed to accomplish?

2. How does this assignment to this committee relate to other assignments to other groups in the agency?

3. How should the committee approach its assignment?

4. What are some of the methods the committee can use to move in on the assignment?

5. What are the specific tasks and the simplest and best ways of performing these tasks?

6. What specific tasks can be assigned to individuals to carry through?

7. What resources are available in the agency and the community to help the committee accomplish its tasks?

8. What materials, facts, are needed by the group?

9. Can the assignment be broken down into parts or steps?

10. What is a realistic and a reasonable time schedule?

11. When must the assignment be completed?

12. What should be done first, second, third, etc.?

13. What kinds of records should be kept?

14. What particular help will be available from the executive as the work goes along?

15. What kind of schedule of conferences and consultations should be worked out between the executive and staff chairman?

NOTES

1. Douglas McGregor, *The Human Side of Enterprise* (New York, N.Y.: McGraw-Hill, 1960), p. 140.

2. *Ibid.,* pp. 47–48.

3. Jay Urice, "Developing and Maintaining an Effective Organization" in Gren O. Pierrel (ed.), *The Executive Role in YMCA Administration* (New York, N.Y.: Association Press, 1951), pp. 110–133.

4. Hedley S. Dimock, "Qualifications of the General Executive Analyzed" in Gren O. Pierrel (ed.), *op. cit.,* pp. 44–45.

5. Roberta Rindfleisch, "Administration of Unmarried Mother Services," *Child Welfare,* December, 1957, p. 28.

6. Robert H. Roy, *The Administrative Process* (Baltimore, Ohio: Johns Hopkins Press, 1958), p. 144.

7. James G. March and Herbert A. Simon, *Organizations* (New York, N.Y.: John Wiley & Sons, 1958), p. 185.

8. Melvin T. Copeland, *The Executive at Work* (Cambridge, Mass.: Harvard University Press, 1952), pp. 143–159.

CHAPTER **10**

Administrative Effectiveness

W_{HAT IS} effective administration? Little formal research has been done on this question in the community
service agency field. Nonetheless, most people have opinions as to whether or not an agency is being administered
in an excellent, good, fair, or poor fashion. Many times
persons have been heard to say, "This is a well-adminis-
tered agency." Others have observed, "When you walk
into this agency you catch the tone and atmosphere of good
management." The reverse may be true. Individuals have
said, "This is poor administration." So one may ask, what
might be the basis for these observations?

Some executives claim that they have never been evaluated and have never really known how effective they were
in their jobs. Nevertheless, they are expected to evaluate

other people, and one may wonder why more attention is not directed toward evaluating administrative leaders themselves.

All too often attempts to appraise administrative effectiveness grow out of crisis situations or are undertaken only when things have gone poorly and the agency is in a confused and threatened state.

Some would argue that it is impossible to evaluate administrative effectiveness because it is made up of such intangible factors that they cannot be measured. Proponents of this position indicate that the best one can hope for is to make value judgments, and under these circumstances the material is hardly reliable. They observe, also, that since administration is an inherent part of the agency you cannot separate out the administrative component, for to do so robs the agency of its wholeness.

These arguments overlook the fact that, planned or unplanned, evaluations of administrative effectiveness are being made. When things go well in the organization the administrator receives a large share of the credit. When things go badly the administrator receives a large share of the blame.

In this chapter the focus will be on measuring administrative effectiveness. The material presented is based upon the assumption that it is possible to single out certain specific executive functions which can be evaluated. How the executive performs these functions is indeed basic to his or her effectiveness and basic to the success of the enterprise. Thus, attention will be focused upon the importance of evaluation and how to go about it.

Importance of Appraising Administrative Effectiveness

There are many inescapable reasons why it is important that attention be given to the continuous appraisal of administrative effectiveness.

First, it is well known that the quality of administrative leadership has a great bearing on the quality of services and programs provided by the agency. When there is good, effective administration there is a far better chance that the program and services will likewise be good.

Second, administrative leaders need to know how well they have done their jobs. They should not be permitted to go on year in and year out without a thoughtful, complete, and accurate assessment of their strengths and their limitations.

Third, appraisal of administrative effectiveness points up the places where administrative leaders need to devise programs of self-improvement and growth. Every person in the human enterprise, including the administrator, needs to establish growth objectives for himself. Thoughtful evaluation is one way of doing this.

Fourth, administrative leaders can receive a great deal of satisfaction from thoughtful appraisal. They are able to see their accomplishments when they are sketched in a time framework. The irritations, frustrations, and disappointments fall aside when a person can stand back and take a considered look at say a year or two of leadership activity.

Fifth, when an agency conscientiously attempts to appraise its administrative strengths it sets the tone for evaluation elsewhere in the agency. When the agency never looks at administration it is obvious that it will be in a vulnerable position when it attempts to appraise other facets of its work.

Sixth, continuous measurement of administrative strengths is of great benefit for the organization as a whole. The organization gets a clear picture of itself. It sees deficiencies that it can remedy. Appraisal highlights the professional strengths and competencies needed at any given time. In the light of these needs, the organization can revise or adapt its administrative approach.

Seventh, administrative appraisal gives perspective to the job and helps the individual see the big task. As Clark and Teall observe, "How often an executive director dashing to the next appointment, hurrying from meeting to meeting, or feverishly shuffling diagrams and reports, has brought herself back to an even keel with the reminder that it is persons who count and that organizational processes must be ordered accordingly."[1]

Eighth, the changing nature of community service agencies makes administrative measurement even more important than it was in an earlier period of history. There have been big changes in the community. There will be even bigger changes in the future. New needs have arisen. New services, new agencies, new methods are here or are on the horizon. In many places communities are questioning the real results of the work done by these agencies. Questions are being raised about their expenditures, and their "efficiency."

There is a growing community component in the job of every administrator. This means that more time is spent on community leadership and community affairs. In addition, there has been a great demand from the community for services. This has brought about an increase in the size of agencies, their expenditures, their needs for facilities and staff, and their needs for leadership. All of these factors are operating today. In addition, staff members and volunteer workers have different expectancies from administrative leaders today. These people want and demand high quality leadership. They expect and they call for stimulation, guidance, and direction. On the other hand, administrators are being asked to co-ordinate a much wider range and variety of professional and technical skills than before. The administrator cannot be everything or do everything. His job is changing. This means that the way he does his job must be looked at again and again.

It is not only important to measure administrative effectiveness and achievement; it is essential that this be done. Unless it is done, how will it ever be possible to determine whether or not agencies are achieving the high goals that they profess?

An Approach to Determining Effectiveness

Executives and board presidents must take a major responsibility for helping their agencies develop a sound and complete approach to the measurement of administrative effectiveness. They must understand the purpose and importance of evaluation and must be strong advocates of its use.

A first step is to determine the basic focus of the appraisal. In the judgment of many authorities the focus of administrative appraisal should be on *job performance* and not on the administrator as a person. Nor should the job be viewed in isolation, but in the framework of what the executive is doing and has done in carrying forward the work that has been assigned to him. Evaluation must be a matter of looking at deeds rather than words. Attention must be directed toward the work of the administrator in the organization as a whole and in terms of the quality of the services rendered by him.

This means that there must be clear job descriptions and clear job assignments and goals for administrative leaders. In addition, there must be agreement as to what is expected from these persons in the way of acceptable accomplishments. Furthermore, appraisal must be related to a particular time period that has been covered and must be regularly scheduled.

Other elements in a systematic plan or approach include answering these questions. Who is to do the evaluating? How is it to be done? What criteria will be used? What is the nature of the evidence sought? How will the findings of evaluation be used? These and other aspects of the problem will be examined in the material which follows.

Who Makes Appraisals?

Appraisals of administrative effectiveness are going on at all times in the human enterprise. They take place in many informal ways and they take place on occasion in the formal channels of the organization. It is generally agreed that the board of the organization is responsible for hiring, helping, evaluating, upgrading, or dismissing the executive. If this is so it is apparent that one of the major responsibilities of the board is to set in motion and carry through a systematic process of administrative appraisal. This function may be delegated to a personnel committee or to a special committee, but such committees are responsible to the board and the board must make ultimate decisions.

The executive of course has the responsibility to provide evaluative material to and for the persons who work with him in a staff capacity, so it goes across the organization. The president has a responsibility to make appraisals of the key administrative volunteers who are carrying forward their share of agency administration.

The staff has a responsibility, too, in participating in the evaluation process. They may do so by solicitation from the executive or they may do so through setting their own goals for their own performance.

Agencies frequently utilize community reaction and reaction from their constituencies or their clients. Material of this kind is exceedingly important if one is to get a complete picture of the impact of administrative leadership.

In some situations the agency utilizes the services of outside consultants. These special consultants may be invited in for a short or long period to make studies of the administrative process and report their findings to the board and staff. Quite often agencies that are affiliated with state or regional or national organizations, both voluntary and governmental, receive help from their field representatives and other special staff members who are in a position to make discriminating judgments in the light of standards and trends.

Perhaps the most important kind of evaluation is that of self-evaluation where through a conscious design and plan administrative leaders look critically at their accomplishments and their weaknesses in relation to a stated period of time and endeavor to draw conclusions as to the ways of strengthening their own performance. A recent publication from the field of education suggests some important questions the administrator may ask if he is concerned about self-evaluation. These questions are "Which tasks deserve the most time? Who can be trusted to make what decisions? Which program should receive the most budget? How can the parts of the system be interrelated? How will staff members react to a given idea? Will this plan foster staff compatability? What is the best way to counsel with the board? How shall a better staff be built?"[2]

How Administrative Leaders View Their Jobs

Authorities in educational administration state, "In the last analysis how an administrator performs on the job will depend mainly on the way he sees his task. . . . The perception of the task is important because how a person performs on his job will depend ultimately upon his view of himself in relation to the work he believes he is commissioned to accomplish. . . . One might say that the school administrator's performance will be largely a matter of his personal value system because he will set his administrative goals accordingly."[3] Thus, a basic prerequisite to the measurement of administrative achievement is to spell out in precise terms the conception of the job that is held by the administrator. "Unless an administrator contemplates his job in its totality he will fall into the rut of relying on short-sighted expedience. Failing to find, or to make, time to look carefully and deeply at the job as a whole, he resorts to the convenient, normally accepted ideas and answers. In order to achieve his purposes the administrator uses a conceptual framework for his job. He is the one person in the organization who is in a position to organize the major processes of decision making on which action can be based. Unless he sees as one of his key roles the patterning of staff resources to serve the organization goals he runs the risk of spending himself on the less consequential demands of his job."[4]

Clark and Teall have specified the three conditions that must be set for the administrator seeking to see the manifold responsibilities of administration as one job. "*First,* the executive director must be seen in relation to each other. . . . When an executive director really accepts the job, she can see what it is and what it is not, she can give herself to its required disciplines. She may like parts of it better than she likes other parts, but it is one job and she can carry it with integrity. She can take satisfaction in it, and others can see what she is trying to accomplish. *Second,* the executive director must give impetus to the formation of objectives, policies and plans, thereby bringing a sense of wholeness to the total operation. . . . *Third,* the executive director must take positive and continuous satisfaction in the work of other people."[5]

The president of a metropolitan YWCA sees her responsibilities in these terms, "The primary job of a president is to lead. That this is done in conjunction with the executive director does not diminish the responsibility or opportunity of either. Joint leadership requires some division of labor; certain areas are the province of the executive, others of the president. But a large middle area must be shared if maximum use is to be made of the leaders. The president must be qualified for her job, as is the executive, and must add constantly to her knowledge, skill and insight. How does a president lead? In her association she constantly presents the triangular relationship between purpose and objective, objective and program, program and purpose. She must preside objectively, but if she doesn't see that certain knowledge is injected into the meeting she does a disservice. She appoints chairmen, listens to them, and helps them act responsibly. She represents her association in the national movement and helps its members know and use the resources offered. She represents her association in the community and listens for opportunities for the YWCA to serve and to add to its assets of leadership and money. She finds ways to relate herself and other professional and volunteer leaders to appropriate community groups and individuals."[6]

The Tools of Measurement

The problem in formulating an accurate assessment of administrative leadership is reduced if an inventory of available tools is made.

Among the tools which are at hand are such things as records, reports, special studies, and other forms of written material. Here are such things as agendas which give evidence of planning, minutes of board and staff meetings, records of follow-up on decisions, preparation material related to the budget, and so on. In addition, there is a substantial amount of impressionistic material which is being presented all of the time as administrative leaders are viewed in their relationships with other people. Here are comments, general judgments, frank statements of appraisal, and the usual day-to-day and month-to-month reactions of people. All of these materials need to be systematically related and organized so that a timely and complete profile can be compiled.

Of great importance is the spelling out of the general and specific criteria which are to be used at any given time.

Criteria of Administrative Effectiveness

In the material which follows an effort will be made to list general criteria which may be used in making an assessment of administrative effectiveness. Some apply to the executive, some to the president, some to other staff and administrative volunteers. It should be pointed out that this lengthy list is offered as a basis for choice and selection. Not all of these criteria will be useful to all agencies. Not all of them will be useful at any one time. Not all of them are of equal importance. Consequently, each agency must draw up for itself a list of those criteria which are most pertinent to its situation at any given time in its history. In making a selection of appropriate criteria, administrative leaders themselves should take responsibility for the major choices.

Inasmuch as they are the ones whose effectiveness is being appraised they must necessarily be involved in determining the criteria which they believe to be representative of their situation.

Goals

1. Effective administrative leaders advance the organization toward its goals of providing high quality programs and services.

2. Effective administrative leaders state and project challenging goals for the period ahead and encourage people to work toward those goals. As Dimock puts it, this calls for an administrator "who can rise above his daily tasks and see his institution with a fresh eye; he is the one capable of providing energy and drive and preventing the onset of decline. Unfortunately many administrators are limited to trouble shooting, to the settling of immediate and often petty crises, and to keeping their noses to the grindstone; as a result, they have no time or energies left over to devote to questions of morale, inspiration, and vitality."[7]

3. Effective administrative leaders have worked out a theory and a philosophy of administration grounded in conviction about democratic values.

4. Effective administrators are conscious of the importance of careful and close control of all finances so that resources will be used to achieve agency purposes.

213

Choosing Personnel and Assigning Work

5. Effective administrators select competent and qualified people and see to it that they are clear on their duties and responsibilities. They surround themselves with the best people they can secure.

6. Effective administrators delegate responsibility to people and show faith in the ability of the people to carry through successfully the assignments they have accepted.

7. Effective administrative leaders make good use of technical resource experts to provide special help on special problems.

Work Organization and Planning

8. Effective administrative leaders handle the mechanics of their job with confidence and dispatch.

9. Effective administrators plan their work carefully. They review their accomplishments and their shortcomings, and they set goals for themselves.

10. Effective administrators think ahead. They concentrate attention on forecasting trends and needs so that the organization will be prepared.

11. Effective administrators predict and anticipate behavior. As a result of their sensitive timing they avoid the creating of situations which arouse misunderstanding and conflict because people are not ready.

12. Effective administrators make good choices in terms of priorities and sequence of items which need to be done at a certain time.

13. Effective administrators know how to handle the unexpected, emergency, crisis situation and know how to deal with the inevitable pressures of work. They are flexible and adaptable and give evidence of being able to respond to the challenge of the moment.

14. Effective administrative leaders spot emerging problems and move in on these problems before they become seriously advanced.

Relationships

15. Effective administrative leaders establish and maintain co-operative, productive, working relationships with their community and their regional and national affiliate groups.

16. Effective administrative leaders achieve a balance in relationships with the board, the staff, the constituency, and the community.

Community

17. Effective administrators seek to understand the continual changing forces of the community, the nation, and the world and keep in mind their over-all responsibility to their community.

18. Effective administrators build good understanding of the services and programs their agency offers through wide and continuous community interpretation.

Leadership

19. Effective administrative leaders give vigorous, continuous, and stimulating leadership to the people with whom they work.

20. Effective administrative leaders concentrate attention upon the growth of persons and the development of leadership. As has been pointed out, "The continued vigor of any institution is dependent in large measure upon its ability to provide a continuous supply of creative leadership to its critical points of control."[8]

21. Effective administrators exhibit a spirit and attitude which is buoyant, hopeful, positive, and contagious, because they know this is an important factor in helping other people achieve their maximum potentials.

22. Effective administrative leaders know how to release the energy of people. As Schlesinger says, "The true test of an administrator may be, not his ability to design and respect organization charts, not his ability to keep within channels, but his ability to concert and release the energies of men for the attainment of public objectives. It might be argued that the essence of successful administration is: First, to acquire the ideas and information necessary for wise decisions; second, to maintain control over the actual making of the decision; and, third, to mobilize men and women who can make the first two things possible. . . ."[9]

Communication and Co-ordination

23. Effective administrative leaders strive to establish good channels of communication within which all members of the organization feel free to contribute their thoughts and energies. This makes for the growth of a responsive staff with high morale.

24. Effective administrative leaders keep people informed about plans, changes, problems, and other important areas of knowledge needed by the total work force.

25. Effective administrative leaders strive to create a sense of organization wholeness and unity. They place accent on the importance of co-ordination of human effort.

Growth

26. Effective administrative leaders give evidence of getting satisfaction out of their work and try to see that others also receive satisfaction.

27. Effective administrative leaders place emphasis on research and evaluation as means of helping them discover better ways of performing their tasks.

28. Effective administrators are oriented toward the future and have learned how to facilitate change within their organization.

29. Effective administrative leaders have worked out a thoughtful program of self-development, including reading and participation in conferences, seminars, and the like.

This matter of administrative leadership development will be considered in the chapter which is to follow.

NOTES

1. Margaret Logan Clark and Briseis Teall, *The Executive Director on the Job* (New York, N.Y.: The Woman's Press, 1947), p. 11.

2. *Professional Administrators for America's Schools,* 38th Yearbook, 1960 (Washington, D.C.: American Association of School Administration, National Education Association), p. 127.

3. *Ibid.,* p. 125.

4. *Ibid.,* p. 140.

5. Clark and Teall, *op. cit.,* pp. 15–17.

6. Harleigh B. Trecker, "Understandings of Administration," *The YWCA Magazine,* June, 1960, p. 26.

7. Marshall E. Dimock, *Administrative Vitality* (New York, N.Y.: Harper & Brothers, 1959), p. 59.

8. *Professional Administrators, op. cit.,* p. 143.

9. Arthur M. Schlesinger, Jr., *The Age of Roosevelt—The Coming of the New Deal,* Vol. II (Boston, Mass.: Houghton-Mifflin Co., 1959), p. 522.

CHAPTER 11

Executive Development

ONE OF THE great needs today is for the establishment of development programs for community service agency executives. Despite the prevalence of such programs in business, industry, and government, up to now the community service field has done little in this important area. It is true that some agencies have limited executive development programs; however, few provide a comprehensive, continuous program. Little is being done to strengthen and augment the skill of present administrative personnel. Not enough opportunities have been created for them to utilize their capacities for growth. Seldom do agencies select and cultivate a pool of potential administrative leaders in sub-positions and provide training for them. In short, community service agencies have neglected executive development.

Importance of Executive Development Program

There are many reasons why community service agencies should give attention to the creation of executive development programs.

First, there has been tremendous growth in the community service field and a large number of administrators are needed now and will be needed in the future. Unless definite steps are taken the present shortage of trained, competent executives will grow even more acute and may reach the crisis stage.

Second, the job of the executive has become more and more complex. There is so much to master and responsibilities are so heavy that even the best of qualified people need constant training and retraining. The executive cannot do his best job on the strength of what was learned in college, or even graduate school, many years ago.

Third, during the last decade or two a tremendous amount of new knowledge has become available. This knowledge should be utilized by executives in carrying forward the administrative process.

Fourth, executives especially need stimulation, new challenges, and opportunities for growth. These can come about better through a formal plan and program of executive development.

Fifth, administrative personnel are a most important human resource. No service, or agency can long expect to provide high quality offerings unless they have administrative leaders who are adequately trained.

Sixth, the changing nature of community services in

both scope and organization requires a constant reappraisal and reinterpretation, especially from the standpoint of modern theories of administration.

Seventh, executive development programs pay for themselves in terms of improved services. Money invested in leadership training is thus a most worthwhile investment.

Planning Executive Development Programs

What must an agency do to plan an adequate program of executive development? Are there steps which can be taken in a systematic fashion? A review of successful executive development programs in other fields clearly indicates that the agency must first think through the importance of training and must create a climate of growth throughout the entire agency. In addition, the agency board together with the executive staff must think through the specific aspects of executive development needs in their agency. They must be committed to the importance of these programs and must think about them in terms of being a continuous requirement and program rather than a single or occasional effort. In other words, executive development must be thought of as an inherent part of good administration. Executive development today is not a luxury but a necessity.

It is suggested that agencies review some of the literature of the field to get some idea of what has been done in terms of executive development programs elsewhere.[1]

It is suggested, also, that the agency get material and assistance from their regional and national offices if they are so affiliated. It is likely that the agency will want to set up a joint committee of board and staff to do the actual planning.

An inventory of present and future needs for executives and sub-executives is an early step to take. It will be necessary then for agencies to analyze positions occupied by executives and sub-executives and to anticipate the number of new positions that will come about in the period ahead. In the preparing of the job analyses the duties, responsibilities, and key skills required should be enumerated. This will allow the agency to focus on the particular knowledge, skills, and attitudes that must be possessed by their top executive leaders.

In the light of these skill needs, an evaluation of present personnel will then be required as a means of locating primary training requirements. While this is being made there should be a study of potential personnel with executive capacity to ascertain their skill levels and to determine the points where they need help. The foregoing steps will lead to a development of suggested areas of content and preparation of material. It will then be possible to give consideration to methods of teaching and to the procedures of selecting specific trainees. Obviously, it will be necessary for agencies to arrange for released time on a scheduled basis so that properly chosen present executives or potential executives may take advantage of the available offerings. Furthermore, the participants themselves must have a voice in spelling out the objectives of training, the areas of content that are most important, and the method of presentation. It has been pointed out many times that the method used in developing the plan is perhaps as important as the content. This is the basic principle of participation which is fundamental to all good administration.

Another underlying principle is the fact that there must be clear goals and objectives if the programs are to be effective. Content should be based on the reality of the present job of the executive and at the same time it should place emphasis upon future needs and future trends. Content should be intellectually stimulating and at the same time should provide opportunity for skill practice in the "doing" aspects of the job.

Inasmuch as time is always limited, there must be a careful selection of content always focused upon the greatest need of the participating group. In addition, it is important to emphasize that good programs are usually tested by way of follow-up evaluation to see the extent to which the objectives have been achieved. In the final analysis executive development is always self-development and the real test is whether or not the experience enables the executive to think more analytically and to perform his tasks with a greater degree of skill and competence.

Objectives of Development Programs

When the agency begins to formulate a program of executive development it must make some judgment as to the characteristics, qualities, and skills of a good executive. The fundamental role of the executive development is, of course, to increase executive effectiveness. This means that having participated in the program the person should be expected to acquire knowledge, attitudes, and skills. The executive thus knows more, thinks differently, and does things differently as a result of this training.

In what area do executives need training? The answer to this question will depend upon who they are, what they have done, what they are doing, and what their jobs demand. The two general primary objectives of most programs are to increase the ability of the executive to understand human motivations and learn how to deal more effectively with people, and second, to increase the ability of the executive to analyze situations and see the alternatives which present themselves as a forerunner to decision making. In addition, the program should provide the means for the executive to keep in touch with developments in his field and should introduce him to new and advanced thinking. To a great extent the most important contribution made by these programs is to help the executive develop new ways of thinking about and approaching tasks. As he gets a deeper understanding of his role and responsibility he is able to study and analyze problems and evaluate the dynamic forces at work in any situation. Thus one of the major goals is to enable the executive to deepen his technical and professional knowledge, sharpen his skills of leadership, delegation, decision making, planning, and the over-all skill of co-ordination of effort.

Avenues of Development

There are many avenues which may be followed in the executive development. Among those that can be considered are, first, formal study in universities and colleges, either by way of advanced programs leading to higher degrees or through taking selective courses during the school year or during summer school. There is a great advantage in the formal study program because colleges and universities can make available a systematic body of knowledge and, of course, a trained and competent faculty. A second avenue is through seminars, institutes, workshops, or short courses developed by a single agency or several agencies or by a university. These concentrated training events have the advantage of requiring less released time from the job and can become extremely valuable in stimulating executives to new ways of thinking about their responsibilities and to new approaches to their work. A third avenue is through conferences and special meetings planned by the agency or by several agencies working together. Conferences have a distinct place in sharpening up the skills of the executive and in helping him to visualize areas for further study.

Some agencies have developed the program of the sabbatical leave which makes it possible for the executive to be away from the job for a stated period after so many years of service. While this development has not been extensive it should be encouraged. Sabbatical leaves provide opportunities for carefully planned study programs which allow the executive to go deeply into areas of basic administrative theory. On-the-job training never permits this kind of reflection and analysis.

Executives should be encouraged to do an increasing amount of self-study. They should be given time to prepare professional papers for presentation at meetings. They should make analytical studies of their own administrative practices based on records that they have kept. They should develop a program of reading and should come together informally with their colleagues in round-table discussions.

A few agencies have worked out programs of executive internships and exchange programs whereby such executives may learn under the guidance and leadership of an experienced director. This, too, represents an avenue for executive development which should be more fully utilized. Pre-induction and orientation training for the new executive is of great importance. As the new worker shifts from direct service to administrative responsibilities there are many areas of learning which are required.

Another avenue is through the progressive enlargement of duties and responsibilities of sub-executives. This kind of procedure has the advantage of gradually increasing the responsibilities of the person so that over a period of time he may enlarge his competency. Some agencies develop a careful plan of assigning their beginning executives to important committees so that they will have this kind of experience under the supervision of the chief executive. Other agencies have a program of staff assistants for the executive so that their future leader may have firsthand experiences.

Up to now the community service field has not established an executive development center. It is to be hoped that eventually governmental and voluntary agencies in the community service field may come together and establish such a center in co-operation with a university, so that a comprehensive and continuous program may be available at all times.

Teaching Methods

Teaching methods for executive development are the same as are found in any educational experience. They include lecture presentations and discussions, reading assignments, written projects, seminar discussions and problem solving through the case analysis method. More and more use is being made of audio-visual materials, demonstrations, and role playing. Among the more productive methods used today is the case analysis method, whereby actual case situations are presented, discussed, and analyzed in relation to the dynamics of the situation and the administrative skills involved in dealing with the situation. Some agencies have developed case materials for training purposes; however, in the community service field this has not progressed to any considerable extent. It means then that material must be adapted from other fields.

It is extremely important for agencies to have a well-planned library of technical and professional materials in administration. Books, pamphlets, reports, and periodicals should be made available so that each executive can work out a personal reading program. In addition, the use of manuals, bulletins, and newsletters can further augment the supply of reading matter which can concentrate attention upon administrative affairs.

Effects of Executive Development

It is to be expected that one of the major results of an executive development program would be that administrators have learned new approaches to their work and have learned how to analyze the situations that confront them. In addition, these programs should result in a better use of the time of present executives and at the same time help to provide a reserve of executive personnel for the future. It should also be observed that when the agencies have definite programs on executive development, this tends to attract much needed younger personnel for the future. When young workers see an opportunity to grow and progress in their jobs they are more likely to be willing to affiliate with such an agency.

What About the Development of Administrative Volunteers?

More and more agencies are realizing that it is also important to have training programs for administrative volunteers such as presidents, other officers, committee chairmen, and board members. To a great extent these training efforts have become regularized in the planning and operation of many agencies. In addition, groups of agencies under the leadership of community planning bodies often come together for community-wide board member preparation. Inasmuch as in the community service field professional workers and administrative volunteers are working together it is important to provide learning experiences which may be shared and which may focus upon common needs and common problems of these two groups.

While little has been done in the area of executive development up to now, it is to be hoped that during the decade ahead substantial gains will be made and that the community service enterprise will do a thorough and outstanding job. This task looms large in terms of needs and desirability. In the closing chapter which is to follow, thought will be given to some of the new frontiers of administration.

NOTES

1. For example, see:

Andrews, Kenneth T., *The Case Method of Teaching Human Relations and Administration* (Cambridge, Mass.: Harvard University Press, 1953).

Bower, Marion, *The Development of Executive Leadership* (Cambridge, Mass.: Harvard University Press, 1951).

Bursk, Edward C., *How to Increase Executive Effectiveness* (Cambridge, Mass.: Harvard University Press, 1954).

Cleeton, Glen U., and Mason, Charles W., *Executive Ability—Its Discovery and Development* (Yellow Springs, Ohio: 1946).

Dooker, W. Joseph (ed.), *The Development of Executive Talent* (New York, N.Y.: American Management Association, 1952).

Livingston, Robert T., and Waite, William W., *The Manager's Job* (New York, N.Y.: Columbia University Press, 1960).

Morell, R. W., *Managerial Decision-Making* (Milwaukee, Wis.: Bruce Publishing Co., 1960).

Riegel, John W., *Executive Development* (Ann Arbor, Mich.: University of Michigan, 1952).

Uris, Auren, *Developing Your Executive Skills* (New York, N.Y.: McGraw-Hill, 1955).

CHAPTER **12**

New Frontiers for Administration

As ADMINISTRATIVE LEADERS, both professional and
volunteer, have moved into the current decade they have
been faced with many challenges and opportunities. Some
of these challenges were presented in the opening chapter.
Now, in closing it may be helpful to suggest an agenda for
the future. What are the frontiers of administration? The
suggestions which are offered in the material to follow
are, of course, speculative. Nevertheless, it is reasonable
to presume that the nation's administrators of the community service enterprise will be concentrating their attention on some if not all of these items.

Adequacy of Services

Administrators will strive to bring about more adequate
services both in terms of availability and of quality. Long

hampered by insufficient funds for personnel, facilities, and equipment, administrators must make vigorous efforts to create a climate in which support for adequate services will be forthcoming. In this connection executives, presidents, chairmen of commissions and advisory groups will have a major role to play in developing better broad public understanding of human needs in a revolutionary world and better understanding of the kinds of services which must be made available to meet these needs.

Sound Public Policy

Administrators will be called upon to take leadership in helping people to think through and formulate sound public policy regarding the responsibilities of the various levels of government and the voluntary agencies. There are many issues to be resolved in this area. Much statesmanlike thinking will be required. The responsibility of the individual in an interdependent society must be related to the responsibility of voluntary effort and government. Without question, much thought will have to be given to the redefinition of agency function and the reallocation of responsibility.

Accent on Prevention

Millions of dollars are spent each year on programs designed to correct individual and social breakdown. These expenditures are necessary. Yet, there is much knowledge available which could be used to prevent the tragic individual and social costs of maladjustment. Consequently administration must place a great accent on prevention as a primary goal for the period ahead. Accumulated knowledge must be put to work and every effort must be made to create the kind of society which will enable all people to reach their fullest potential.

Evaluation of Services

Administrators must take more responsibility for making critical evaluations of existing services. This will call for a sharper focusing of objectives, careful gathering of evidence, definite drafting of evaluative criteria, and courageous willingness to face up to shortcomings. There is a great need for critical evaluation of all programs, the large public ones as well as the smaller voluntary ones. Some agencies have been in existence for a long time without giving sufficient attention to a factual facing of how well they are achieving their goals. Some agencies may need a critical overhauling in terms of purpose and program. Here administrators face both an obligation and an opportunity.

Co-ordination and Planning

The growth of agencies and services in the past half century has been unparalleled in all history. Unfortunately, much of the growth has been carried forward without regard to over-all planning. As a consequence there is some competition between agencies, duplication of effort, and gaps between agencies which should be closed. In the light of this situation administrators must give considerable attention to what goes into better co-ordination and planning of services. This will require new insights of interagency working relationships, new depths of understanding of interdisciplinary approaches, and in some cases the merger of agencies and the consolidation of services. These efforts must be made to bring about a better meeting of current needs and a more planful approach to the future.

Geographic Areas Served

The network of community agencies that has developed in the past half century covers many different geographical areas ranging from the small neighborhood to the state-wide or region-wide complex. Challenging questions of efficiency and economy are being raised in this mobile society with its ever present shifting population. Administration thus faces a major task in reviewing the present geographic basis used for the distribution of services. While there is no easy answer to this problem it is evident that administrative leaders must take responsibility for a critical re-drawing of the lines of service.

Understanding the Agency

Inasmuch as the methods and processes of administration must be related to that which is being administered, it will be increasingly necessary for administrative leaders to deepen their understanding of the community service agency and its particular sub-cultural aspects. What are the unique properties or characteristics of these many agencies? What patterns of conduct, belief, and values underlie their

233

establishment and continuation? It is no longer sufficient for administrators to say "our agencies are different." They must spell out in clearer detail those facets of agency operations which demand and require unique professional processes and sub-processes.

Manpower Resources Needed

During the past decade perhaps the most pressing problem faced by all administrators has been the manpower problem. There is general acceptance of the fact that high standard professional services cannot be provided without a qualified professional staff. The shortage of qualified people has been serious and is likely to grow more serious. Thus administration must quickly review all manpower procedures designed to recruit, select, utilize, and retain well-prepared staff members. National conferences dealing with children and youth and the aged have agreed that a central concern is that of manpower. Governmental and voluntary forces under the leadership of administrators must face this critical problem with unceasing effort if solutions are to be found.

Executive Job Study

Every executive must give more thought and study to his own job and his own use of time and energy. A universal complaint of all executives is their failure to find time to think, reflect, and project their plans into the future. Evidently strong efforts must be made to separate the professional and technical content of the job from the routine and non-professional content. This may call for development of a category of workers to be known as general administrative aides, who will thus free chief executives for the more vigorous prosecution of their leadership role. In addition, a great deal of work will be done on the early selection, training, and placement of young executives, who will be given major leadership tasks in the future.

Data Processing Methods

Administrators will find it necessary to explore and seek to utilize modern methods of data processing. During recent years a whole new technology of data recording and analysis has emerged. These new devices for computing and analyzing have scarcely been utilized in the community service field. Every effort should be made to modernize processes and procedures which will provide instant data for both service and fiscal controls.

Facts and Forecasting

Administrators, during the period ahead, will give special attention to the continuous collection and analysis of factual data so essential in forecasting and in program planning. Large agencies may definitely require specialized personnel to secure, collate, and analyze the social data needed to make sound administrative decisions. Community planning bodies, through their research staffs, can be of great assistance in this regard. Projecting needs and forecasting developments will loom larger in the leadership responsibility of the administrator.

Clarification of Policy Making

Administrators will give more attention to the continuous clarification of policy-making processes and responsibilities as distinguished from day-to-day management and operation. Careful studies of policies, their history, and development, will bring about a more complete understanding of the policy-making process which is so essential today.

Administration Theory Formulation

Much work needs to be done in deepening our knowledge and understanding of administration as a process. Theories of community service agency administration are in the beginning stages of formulation. Much can be learned from exploring the common elements in community service administration, business administration, and public administration. New dimensions of organization theory are being probed by social scientists. It is to be hoped that the scientists and the administrators will enter into closer communication so that administrative theory formulation will move ahead.

Research in Administration

The graduate schools of social work in our universities, working in co-operation with community agencies, must formulate and seek support for a long-range, continuing program of research in social administration. While this will be difficult and expensive the results from such research will undoubtedly prove the soundness of both time and money expenditures.

Summary

The fourteen points outlined above present an unparalleled opportunity for all administrators who would exercise leadership in efforts designed to shape the future of the human services. The facts are beyond dispute. The new frontiers of administration are clearly visible. To penetrate their boundaries, to explore their possibilities, to develop their potentialities is the great task of progressive administrators everywhere.

Bibliography of Selected Readings

Abrahamson, Arthur C. *Group Methods in Supervision and Staff Development*. New York: Harper & Brothers, 1959.

Appley, Lawrence A. *Management in Action*. New York: American Management Association, 1956.

Argyris, Chris. *Personality and Organization—The Conflict Between System and the Individual*. New York: Harper & Brothers, 1957.

————. "The Organization: What Makes It Healthy?" *Harvard Business Review*, November–December, 1958.

Aronson, Albert. "The Application of Business Techniques to the Administration of a Social Agency," in *Administration, Supervision, and Consultation*. Papers from the 1954 Social Welfare Forum, National Conference of Social Work. New York: Family Service Association, 1955.

Baldwin, Joseph E. "Applying Management Principles to Public Welfare Administrators," *Social Service Review*, March, 1957.

Barnard, Chester I. *The Functions of the Executive*. Cambridge: Harvard University Press, 1938 or 1950.

Bass, Bernard M. *Leadership, Psychology and Organizational Behavior*. New York: Harper & Brothers, 1960.

Bennis, Warren G. "Leadership Theory and Administrative Behavior," *Administrative Science Quarterly*, December, 1959.

Better Boards and Committees. (Leadership Pamphlet No. 14.) Chicago: Adult Education Association, U.S.A., 1957.

Blackey, Eileen A. *Group Leadership in Staff Training.* Washington, D.C.: U.S. Department of Health, Education, and Welfare, Children's Bureau and Bureau of Public Assistance, 1957.

Blum, Fred. "Social Audit of the Enterprise," *Harvard Business Review,* March–April, 1958.

Brownrigg, William. *The Human Enterprise Process.* University: University of Alabama Press, 1954.

Campbell, Donald T. *Leadership and Its Effects Upon the Group.* (Business Research Monograph No. 83.) Columbus: Ohio State University, 1956.

Campbell, Roald F., and Gregg, Russell T. (eds.). *Administrative Behavior in Education.* New York: Harper & Brothers, 1957.

Cantor, Nathaniel. *The Learning Process for Managers.* New York: Harper & Brothers, 1958.

Caudill, William. *The Psychiatric Hospital as a Small Society.* Cambridge: Harvard University Press, 1958.

Clapp, Gordon R. "The Social Scientist and the Administrative Art," in *The State of the Social Sciences,* Leonard D. White (ed.). Chicago: The University of Chicago Press, 1956.

Cloward, Richard A. "Agency Structure as a Variable in Service to Groups," in *Group Work and Community Organization,* National Conference on Social Welfare. New York: Columbia University Press, 1956.

Cohen, Nathan E. *Social Work in the American Tradition.* New York: Dryden Press, 1958.

———. *The Citizen Volunteer.* New York: Harper & Brothers, 1960.

Crookes, Spencer H. "Administrative Responsibility for Planning," *Child Welfare,* October, 1957.

Cruickshank, Henry M., and Davis, Keith. *Case Studies in Management.* Homewood, Ill.: Richard D. Irwin, Inc., 1958.

Culbertson, Jack A., et al. *Administrative Relationships—A Casebook.* Englewood Cliffs, N.J.: Prentice-Hall Inc., 1960.

Dimock, Marshall E. *Administrative Vitality—The Conflict with Bureaucracy.* New York: Harper & Brothers, 1959.

Bibliography

————. *A Philosophy of Administration—Toward Creative Growth.* New York: Harper & Brothers, 1958.

Dooker, M. Joseph (ed.). *The Development of Executive Talent.* New York: American Management Association, 1952.

Dorsey, John T. "A Communication Model for Administration," *Administrative Science Quarterly,* December, 1957.

Drucker, Peter F. *The Practice of Management.* New York: Harper & Brothers, 1954.

Dubin, Robert. *Human Relations in Administration.* New York: Prentice-Hall, 1951.

Ewing, David W. (ed.). *Long-range Planning for Management.* New York: Harper & Brothers, 1958.

Ginsberg, Eli, et al. *Effecting Change in Large Organizations.* New York: Columbia University Press, 1957.

Glover, John B., and Hower, Ralph M. *The Administrator.* Homewood, Ill.: Richard D. Irwin, Inc., 1952.

Golembiewski, Robert T. "The Small Group and Public Administration," *Public Administration Review,* Summer, 1959.

Gouldner, Helen P. "Dimensions of Organizational Commitment," *Administrative Science Quarterly,* March, 1960.

Grundstein, Nathan D. "Understanding Self and Organization," *Public Administration Review,* Autumn, 1958.

Haire, Mason (ed.). *Modern Organization Theory.* New York: John Wiley & Sons, 1959.

Halpin, Andrew W. (ed.). *Administrative Theory in Education.* Chicago: Midwest Administration Center, University of Chicago, 1958.

Hanchette, Helen, et al. *Some Dynamics of Social Agency Administration.* New York: Family Service Association, 1946.

Hodges, Wayne. *Company and Community—Case Studies in Industry-City Relationships.* New York: Harper & Brothers, 1958.

Houle, Cyril O. *The Effective Board.* New York: Association Press, 1960.

Johns, Ray. *Executive Responsibility.* New York: Association Press, 1954.

Jones, Manley Howard. *Executive Decision Making.* Homewood, Ill.: Richard D. Irwin, Inc., 1957.

Katz, Robert L. "Skills of an Effective Administrator," *Harvard Business Review,* January–February, 1955.

———. "Steps in Determining Effective Administrative Action," *Advanced Management,* February, 1959.

———. "Toward a More Effective Enterprise," *Harvard Business Review,* September–October, 1960.

Koontz, Harold, and O'Donnell, Cyril. *Principles of Management— An Analysis of Managerial Functions.* New York: McGraw-Hill, 1955.

Kruse, Arthur H. "Administration of Social Welfare Agencies," in *Social Work Yearbook,* 1960 (ed.). Russell Kurtz, New York: National Association of Social Workers, 1960.

Laird, Donald A., and Laird, Eleanor C. *The Techniques of Delegating.* New York: McGraw-Hill, 1957.

Lawrence, Paul R. *The Changing of Organizational Behavior Patterns.* Boston: Harvard University Graduate School of Business Administration, 1958.

Leavitt, Harold J. *Managerial Psychology.* Chicago: University of Chicago Press, 1958.

Likert, Rensis. "Measuring Organizational Performance," *Harvard Business Review,* March–April, 1958.

Mandelbaum, Arthur. "Psychological Obstacles to Communications," in *Toward Understanding Men.* Topeka: The Menninger Foundation, 1957.

March, James G., and Simon, Herbert A. *Organizations.* New York: John Wiley & Sons, 1958.

Martin, Norman H. "Strategy in Administrative Action," *Hospital Administration,* Spring, 1958.

McGregor, Douglas. *The Human Side of Enterprise.* New York: McGraw-Hill, 1960.

Merrill, Harwood F. *Classics in Management.* New York: American Management Association, 1960.

Metcalf, Henry C., and Urwick, L. (eds.). *Dynamic Administration— The Collected Papers of Mary Parker Follett.* New York and London: Harper & Brothers, 1942.

Moss, Celia R. *Administering a Hospital Social Service Department.* New York: National Association of Social Workers, 1955.

242

Bibliography

Neighborhood Goals in a Rapidly Changing World. New York: National Federation of Settlements and Neighborhood Centers, 1958.

Newman, William H. *Administrative Action—The Techniques of Organization and Management.* New York: Prentice-Hall, 1951.

Norris, Louis William, "Moral Hazards of an Executive," *Harvard Business Review,* September–October, 1960.

Osborn, Phyllis R. "Meeting the Needs of People: An Administrative Responsibility," *Social Work,* July, 1958.

Personnel Administration in a Girl Scout Council. New York: Girl Scouts of U.S.A., 1957.

Pfiffner, John M. "Administrative Rationality," *Public Administration Review,* Summer, 1960.

———, and Sherwood, Frank P. *Administrative Organization.* Englewood Cliffs, N.J.: Prentice-Hall, 1960.

Pierrel, Gren O. *The Executive Role in YMCA Administration.* New York: Association Press, 1951.

Professional Administrators for America's Schools. (Thirty-eighth Yearbook, 1960.) Washington, D.C.: American Association of School Administrators, National Education Association.

The Public Welfare Board Member and His Unique Role. Chicago: American Public Welfare Association, 1958.

Ransohoff, Priscilla B. "The Administrator and Management Development," *Hospital Administration,* Winter, 1958.

Redfield, Charles E. *Communication in Management.* Chicago: University of Chicago Press, 1953.

Riegel, John W. *Executive Development.* Ann Arbor: University of Michigan, Bureau of Industrial Relations, 1952.

Ronken, Harriet, and Lawrence, Paul R. *Administering Changes.* Boston: Harvard University School of Business Administration, 1952.

Rose, Albert. "Coordination in Physical and Social Planning in a Metropolitan Area," *Social Service Review,* December, 1958.

Rosen, Ephraim. "The Executive Personality," *Personnel,* January–February, 1959.

Ross, Murray, and Hendry, Charles E. *New Understandings of Leadership.* New York: Association Press, 1957.

Roy, Robert H. *The Administrative Process.* Baltimore: Johns Hopkins, Press, 1958.

Ryan, Margaret. "Professional-Volunteer-Client Interrelationships," in *Social Work with Groups,* 1959. Selected Papers from the National Conference on Social Welfare. New York: National Association of Social Workers, 1959.

Schmidt, William D. *The Executive and the Board in Social Welfare.* Cleveland: Howard Allen, Inc., 1959.

Seckler-Hudson, Catheryn. *Organization and Management: Theory and Practice.* Washington, D.C.: The American University Press, 1955.

Selznick, Philip. *Leadership in Administration—A Sociological Interpretation.* Evanston: Row, Peterson & Co., 1957.

Simon, Herbert A. *Administrative Behavior.* New York: Macmillan Co., 1958.

———. "The Administrator as a Decision-Maker," *Hospital Administration,* Spring, 1958.

Smith, George Albert. *Managing Geographically Decentralized Companies.* Boston: Harvard University Graduate School of Business Administration, 1958.

Spencer, Sue W. *The Administration Method in Social Work.* (Curriculum Study on Social Work Education, Vol. III.) New York: Council on Social Work Education, 1959.

Stein, Harold. *Public Administration and Policy Development—A Case Book.* New York: Harcourt Brace & Co., 1952.

Stogdill, Ralph M., and Shartle, Carroll L. *Methods in the Study of Administrative Leadership.* (Research Monograph No. 80, Bureau of Business Research.) Columbus: Ohio State University, 1955.

Summer, Charles E., Jr. *Factors in Effective Administration.* New York: Columbia University Graduate School of Business, 1956.

Tead, Ordway. *Administration: Its Purpose and Performance.* New York: Harper & Brothers, 1959.

———. *The Art of Administration.* New York: McGraw-Hill, 1951.

Thomas, Edwin J., et al. *In-Service Training and Reduced Workloads—Experiments in a State Department of Welfare.* New York: Russell Sage Foundation, 1960.

Thompson, James D. "Organizational Management of Conflict," *Administrative Science Quarterly,* March, 1960.

————, et al. *Comparative Studies in Administration.* Pittsburgh: University of Pittsburgh Press, 1959.

Urwick, L. F. *Leadership in the 20th Century.* New York: Pitman, 1957.

————. *The Pattern of Management.* Minneapolis: University of Minnesota Press, 1956.

Vasey, Wayne. "Partnership between Administrator and Staff in Developing Sound Welfare Programs," *Social Casework,* April, 1952.

Walton, John. *Administration and Policy-Making in Education.* Baltimore: Johns Hopkins Press, 1959.

Weiss, Robert L. *Processes of Organization.* Ann Arbor: University of Michigan, Survey Research Center, Institute for Social Research, 1956.

Zaleznik, A. *The Motivation, Productivity and Satisfaction of Workers.* Boston: Harvard School of Business Administration, 1959.

Seven Day's

DATE DUE

7 DAY BOOK	This book may be kept for 7 days only It cannot be renewed	
Summer		
OC 31 '78		
DEC 1 4 1981		
AP 19 '94		
GAYLORD		PRINTED IN U.S.A.